Vote for Jesus

How to preach effectively

David E. Flavell

Kevin
Mayhew

First published in 2002 by
KEVIN MAYHEW LTD
Buxhall, Stowmarket, Suffolk IP14 3BW
E-mail: info@kevinmayhewltd.com

9 8 7 6 5 4 3 2 1 0

ISBN 1 84003 848 9
Catalogue No 1500474

Cover design by Angela Selfe
Edited by Katherine Laidler
Typesetting by Louise Selfe
Printed in Great Britain

Acknowledgements

I would like to thank the following people for helping with the manuscript: Martha Tracy Flavell, Elaine Standish, Rob Eastaway, Neville and Pam Flavell, Chris and Fiona Hewitt, Marie Dove, Ross Tracy, Ross and Julie O'Neal, Chris McCoy, Liz Bates, Katherine Laidler, David MacDonald and David Rogerson.

I would like to thank Dennis Ashton, Revd Bob Dickinson, and Marion Hawley for the work they did in helping administer the 'question' survey.

The cartoons were drawn by Dik La Pine and Andrew Fox.

About the author

David Flavell is a Methodist minister in Liverpool. He has been a preacher for more than 12 years and he hopes he has improved during that time. Since his first sermon lasted nearly an hour and went from Genesis to Revelation and back again, that shouldn't be a difficult goal.

He is married with two daughters and a black labrador. When his wife was asked, 'Have you ever thought of being a preacher?' she responded that she already had enough preaching to do at home.

David is convinced of at least three things:

1. That preaching can make a difference.
2. That the Church will change.
3. That Sheffield United are destined for the Premiership.

He is the author of two other successful books, *Cooking Up Worship* and *Getting Married in Church – Again*, also published by Kevin Mayhew.

David's next project is his first novel.

Ballot paper

Dedicated to the memory of Phillips Brooks

Introduction

Lectures inform; talks entertain; sermons persuade.

This book is written for preachers, but some of the principles it contains would be useful for anybody who needs to engage in public speaking. It is no coincidence that many trade union leaders and politicians gained their first experience as lay preachers. Over the years I have heard criticism of sermons and the dullness of the Church, but in my experience of sitting and listening the average quality of sermons is far better than the average quality of speeches and lectures. The world still has much to learn from the Church.

In this book, those new to preaching will find a complete blueprint from start to finish as to how to write a sermon. Instruction is combined with humour, and there are hints and tips to help preachers learn their craft.

Those of you who are experienced preachers will discover new approaches to sermon content and construction that could revolutionise the effectiveness of your preaching.

Vote for Jesus is a resource that is straightforward enough to be read at one sitting, but can be dipped into again and again. May it inform you; may it entertain you; but most of all may it *persuade* you to try something new.

I hope you enjoy reading it.

Revd David E. Flavell
Http://www.evoevo.pwp.blueyonder.co.uk

Chapter 1

The election campaign

A sermon is like a party political broadcast. Why is this?

1. People switch off when they know one is coming.

2. The aim is for people to put the cross in the right place.

3. The 'result' matters more than the 'performance'.

4. The best ones make them say, 'My God, that's absolutely right!'

5. The worst are talking-heads droning on about technical issues.

6. Honesty is the best policy.

7. You need to aim for the 'swing-voter' each time.

8. The faithful are encouraged when they hear the message repeated.

9. Some people have already made their mind up before you begin.

10. The cumulative effect of several presentations is likely to have more effect than one single go.

11. The response, 'That was very interesting and made me think', is failure.

12. The response, 'I'm going to get out and vote', is success.

Now I'm not saying that sermons *should* be like party political broadcasts. They don't have to follow the same format or the same rules. What I am saying is that sermons have the same *aim* as party political broadcasts. That aim is to spur people into action.

The Christian life is like a prolonged election campaign. Every day, members of the Church have the opportunity to vote for Jesus – or not. We have the choice to deflect that unkind remark in the way that Jesus would, or to be hurtful in response. We have the choice to do something for the least, the last and the lost of this world, or to be complacent. We have the choice to share the Good News with somebody else, or to keep our heads down.

Most of the time we don't recognise that we have a choice to vote for Jesus, because we decided how we would cast our ballots years ago. We are prepared to make the Christian response – up to a point.

There are issues upon which we are entirely with Jesus – of course we should give to charity. There are times when we consider that Jesus asks far too much – give all we have to the poor? You must be joking!

Only occasionally do we come across a moral dilemma where we have to stop and think which way we should cast our vote.

The task of the preacher is to encourage members of the congregation to cast their votes for Jesus. Each time we hear a sermon, there is the opportunity for us to re-evaluate our decisions. When the preacher speaks, we can be persuaded to think again about the way we live our life. Through the sermon, God has the chance to speak to us afresh, and to encourage us to vote for Jesus in *everything we do.*

A party political broadcast is designed to encourage people to vote for the party. It aims to convince the wavering to change their allegiance, and to convince the faithful to get out and use their vote, because every vote counts.

A sermon is designed to encourage the congregation to build the kingdom of God. It aims to convince the wavering to follow Jesus, and to convince the faithful to get out and start working, because every individual counts. Once again God's manifesto is presented to us and we are encouraged to live new lives.

Or at least we should be. Some preachers just give a lecture which *informs* us about the world of the Bible. Other preachers give a talk which *entertains* us, but no more.

Yet the preacher is not a neutral figure. The preacher is there both to inform us and to entertain us, but more than that, to *persuade* us to follow God's way, and to vote for Jesus.

If you are preaching about Jesus asking the disciples, 'Who do you say that I am?', you are not neutral as to the answer. You want to persuade the congregation to say with Peter, 'You are the Christ.' It is that desire to persuade which marks the difference between a preacher and a lecturer.

As a preacher, you need to persuade people to change. You have a short time on a Sunday to call people back to what

is important in life. If you are happy with the way that the world is, and happy with the way that others are casting their votes as Christians, then perhaps you shouldn't be preaching. If you just want to educate and inform, then become a lecturer or teacher. If you want to entertain, join the world of show business.

If you have a passionate desire to change the world, and you think that everyone can make a difference, then preaching is for you, and this book is for you.

Every true politician would rather win elections than awards for the quality of the election broadcasts. It is the result

Spurgeon's conversion

The famous nineteenth-century evangelist, Charles Haddon Spurgeon, was converted by what he described as the worst sermon he ever heard.

It was snowing in Colchester on a Sunday in January 1850, so Spurgeon could not go to his usual church. Instead he went to the Artillery Street Primitive Methodist Chapel, to find a congregation of about 15. The weather was so bad that the preacher didn't turn up, so one of the laymen had to lead the service. He had no training, and apparently he couldn't even pronounce the words properly.

However, his direct appeal to the young man in his congregation to 'look and be saved' worked, and Spurgeon was never the same again. Spurgeon went on to have a tremendous ministry and was regarded as one of the greatest preachers of his day.

That day, it was the result that was important, not the quality of the message.

that counts. Every true preacher would rather see lives changed than be complimented on the quality of their sermon. (See 'Spurgeon's conversion', page 10.)

Each week as a preacher, you have the opportunity to persuade your congregation to vote for Jesus.

Matthew 25:47
My version: The sheep and the goats and the owls

And the owls said, 'We saw you hungry and thirsty and naked and alone, and we thought very deeply about the structural issues involved over lunch, and realised that we could only do something collectively.'

'Great,' said Jesus. 'You were involved in the Third World Debt Campaigns, then?'

'We thought about that too and decided that they were hopelessly compromised because much of the money saved is spent on arms instead.'

Jesus said, 'So you ended up doing nothing? Didn't you hear what I said about those who fail to act in the parable of the talents? My friend Matthew wrote it down in what you call Chapter 25. Didn't you read the bit that says, 'Whoever doesn't have, even the small amount they have will be taken from them. And throw those useless servants into the darkness, where there will be weeping and gnashing of teeth.'?

'Yes, we read that.'

'And?'

'We started pondering: How can a loving God condemn people to hell? It makes you think, doesn't it?'

And Jesus wept.

Vote for Jesus

But what does it actually mean to vote for Jesus? What do you want your listeners to do?

In every sermon, there is the opportunity to spur the congregation to action. As a preacher, you are not there just to entertain or to inform. You can try to persuade the congregation to change the world. A sermon without the expectation of some kind of response is lacking the vital ingredient.

To some preachers, voting for Jesus means becoming a Christian and telling others about your conversion. Voting for Jesus is about evangelism, and they want to persuade you to evangelise. (Matthew 28:19)

To some preachers, voting for Jesus means repenting of your ways and starting a new life. Voting for Jesus is about repentance, and they want to persuade you to repent. (Mark 1:15)

To some preachers, voting for Jesus means standing alongside the poor, and working with the least, the last and the lost. Voting for Jesus is about social action, and they want to persuade you to care for the poor. (Luke 10:25-37)

To some preachers, voting for Jesus means being a witness in your exemplary moral behaviour and following the Ten Commandments. Voting for Jesus is about standing out from the crowd, and they want to persuade you to make that stand. (John 17:13-19)

To some preachers, voting for Jesus means praying for the world and its needs. Voting for Jesus is about spending time in prayer, and they want to persuade you to have quiet time, and to pray and read the Bible. (Matthew 6:1-15)

The point is that we can cast our vote for Jesus in many ways. Whichever passage of scripture we use, there is nearly always something to which we can respond.

Casting a vote is both a physical and a practical action. It is something that we *do*. Jesus calls us to do many things, but we never read of him in the gospels saying, 'I want you to go away and think about that because it's very interesting.'

A preacher has failed if afterwards people say, 'That was really interesting. I'm going to go home and think about it.' A preacher has succeeded if people say, 'I'm going to go home and *do* something about it. Preaching should provoke a response, and that response has to be more than just thinking. Congregations say, 'I like a sermon that makes me think.' Part of the reason for that is that it's easier to think than to act.

A party political broadcast has succeeded if people respond, 'I'm going to go out and vote', and then they physically complete their commitment. It has failed if people say, 'Well, that was really interesting, and made me think about some important issues.'

For every passage of scripture, and for every issue, there is a Christian response. In fact, there are usually several Christian responses. It is not always easy to know what the 'right' response is, and this is where the preacher comes in.

Your job as a preacher is to look at the world as it is, then to look at the world as it should be, and to help the congregation to see how they can get there. The world lives in slavery in Egypt, God wants people to get to the Promised Land, and you are like Moses, having to persuade a stiff-necked people to leave.

Changing the world

Seven commands that Jesus gave

- Be reconciled (Matthew 5:24)
- Take up your cross and deny yourself (Matthew 16:24)
- Forgive (Matthew 18:22)
- Give all your money away (Mark 10:21)
- Heal the sick (Luke 10:9)
- Follow me (John 1:43)
- Love one another (John 13:34)

Isn't it a bit ambitious asking the preacher to be like Moses?

I suppose it is, but preachers are ambitious. We are not here to make mediocre people a little better. We are here to turn the worst of sinners into the greatest of saints.

That doesn't mean, however, that we are constantly asking people to leave their homes and everything to follow Jesus. (Mind you, that's what he did.)

Instead, we remember that the trek from Egypt to the Promised Land began with a single step, and that first step was the hardest one.

When we call people to vote for Jesus, then we should be asking them to do things which are simple, practical and achievable. So, for instance, if you were calling people to vote for Jesus by evangelising you might say:

Today I'm not calling you to become a missionary overseas, although if you were, that would be wonderful, and anybody who feels called to be a missionary, have a word with me afterwards. I'm not calling you to go round knocking on doors around the local streets, although if you did, that would be wonderful and have a word with me afterwards if you want to. Instead I'm calling you to speak to *one* person this week, and to invite them to come to church. It could be a neighbour, a friend, or someone in your family.

Within that paragraph, there are actually three calls. There is the simple, practical and achievable goal of inviting one person. There is the more challenging and scary prospect of knocking on doors. There is also the bigger challenge of becoming a missionary.

This allows for different levels of response, depending on where people are in their Christian life. If your challenges are always dramatic, then you make them too hard for ordinary people to do, and they end up feeling guilty that they're not like St Peter. If your challenges are trivial or too easy, then why bother?

The main aim of this sermon is to get them to vote for Jesus by inviting one person to church, but there are even deeper challenges.

The main aim of a party political broadcast is to encourage the electorate to get out and vote, but always the address of the party is given at the end, should you wish to make a further commitment and join.

By offering several opportunities, you maximise the potential response of the congregation.

Ordering people about

This isn't a question of telling people what to do. Remember, you are trying to *persuade*, and if you are bossy that's going to be counter-productive. All you are doing is outlining an issue, and then suggesting Christian responses which you would like your congregation to make.

If you don't want to be quite so directive, then you can offer more choice to the congregation:

Now maybe you think it is inappropriate to invite somebody to church in response to the call of Jesus to 'go and make disciples of all nations'. That's fine. Instead it would be excellent if you could come up with a more appropriate idea and put it into action this week.

Other preachers

What if somebody else would call people to vote for Jesus in a different way? Is there just one Christian response to each situation?

No, there isn't. Different preachers have different ideas, but God can still work through them. Just because other preachers would call people to vote for Jesus in another way doesn't mean that you should give up.

God has called you to be a preacher, and wants to use you to speak to others. You are not trying to persuade the congregation that your way is the *only* Christian way. You are saying that you want the congregation to vote for Jesus, and this is one very good way of doing it.

What about next week?

Next week we will want people to vote for Jesus again. There will be another subject and another call. It may even be by another preacher. We don't just want people to vote once and then forget about it. Instead, each week we want to offer the opportunity to vote for Jesus again.

Each time we preach we have to work once again at getting folk to vote for Jesus. Like St Paul, we have to do all that we can, becoming like a Jew to the Jews, like a Gentile to the Gentiles, weak to the weak and strong to the strong in order that we might win some.

Short time available

When King Agrippa met the imprisoned Paul in Acts 26, he said, 'Surely you don't think that in such a short time you can persuade me to be a Christian?'

And Paul responds, 'Whether it's a short time or a long time, I hope all of you become Christians exactly like me – apart from the chains I'm wearing.'

As preachers, we have the advantage of not being in chains, but we do have the same job as St Paul: a short time to persuade people to vote for Jesus.

Before I get to the subject of my sermon, which won't be for some time . . .

Chapter 2

How are people persuaded?

How can you influence people to your way of thinking?

The first thing to say is that the best way *not* to do it is to shout at them. The days are long gone when the person in the pulpit could say, 'This is the way the Church thinks and this is the way you must think without question.' If the preacher does say that, then the congregation reacts against it.

Instead, people are persuaded by:

- rational argument
- teaching
- friends
- love
- respect
- their emotions
- their instincts
- clarity
- honesty and integrity
- humility
- an attractive presentation
- a good worship experience
- lack of cynicism
- personal testimony
- relevance
- the Holy Spirit

We'll go through these one by one.

Rational argument

Proof texts

Preaching is not a proof, nor an essay which concludes with the answers. If you want that, then get *Mere Christianity* by C. S. Lewis, an excellent explanation of the Gospel even today. You can find it in the resources section in Chapter 13.

Many sermons are written on the basis that if you provide a rational logical argument that is put together well, then people will have no option but to agree with the preacher. Now that may be true of an essay, but preaching is not essay writing.

With an essay you can always go back if you don't understand a point, and read it again. With a sermon if you disagree or don't hear, then there is no way of starting again.

The most wonderful, thoughtful, logical sermon can fall flat on its face because the listeners have missed the first point which is crucial to making sense of all the others.

Teaching

Closely allied to rational argument is the idea that we believe what we are taught. This is to some extent true, but I want to argue that preaching a sermon is a very bad way of teaching a lesson. I would go so far as to say that a 'teaching sermon' is a contradiction in terms.

Classic teaching theory and the sermon can only travel so far together. They both begin the same way. See the table.

for the students to practise, followed by the marking of the papers to make sure they have understood.

But at the end of the sermon, the crucial difference is the missing follow-up. It is impossible to know if the lessons have been learnt. It would be wonderful if there could be guided and unguided

Teaching Theory	*Explanation*	Preaching
Anticipatory set – A loaf to talk about the Corn Laws.	*Anticipatory set – the 'catch' at the start that gets the attention.*	Anticipatory set – A loaf to talk about communion.
Tell them what you will say.		Tell them what you will say.
Say it.		Say it.
Tell them what you've said.	*Repetitive technique to reinforce the lesson.*	Tell them what you've said.
Guided practice	*Help the students with examples.*	None
Unguided practice	*Let the students have a go on their own.*	None
Assessment	*Mark the papers to see if they have understood.*	None

At the start of a lesson *and* of a sermon, there is usually some special opening gambit to catch the attention, and to make people want to listen further.

Then in a lesson *and* in a sermon, the message is given, often in a repetitive manner to drill it home.

At the end of a lesson, there is the time

practice, and even better if there could be assessment, but realistically this is not going to happen in the context of a sermon. Nor is there normally the opportunity for follow-up questions.

This is not to say that there shouldn't be teaching in the Church. I think it is vital that we teach. Many of the people in our congregations are not sure what the Bible says, and what it means.

The place to find out is in Bible studies, and I think it is no coincidence that groups like Alpha and Disciple have been so popular. This is because you can ask questions and interact, rather than just listen. More than that, you recap what happened last time, and what has been going on in the last week, which is similar to the model of guided practice – unguided practice – assessment.

How long, O Lord?

In the old days, you were advised to spend an hour of study for each minute of the sermon.

With modern technological advances (see Chapter 11), there is more flexibility.

Every preacher knows the dreaded 'Saturday night slog' of having to produce a sermon, but ideally it should be completed well before.

Some preachers are disciplined enough to have their sermons ready a month beforehand.

A good practice is to look at your material at least a week before your sermon. Then you can allow your thoughts to 'brew'. During the week you can come across relevant illustrations.

When it comes to the time to write the sermon, hopefully it will just 'flow'. This doesn't always happen, but when it does, you know you are on the right lines.

Friends

You are much more likely to persuade somebody you know than you would a stranger. If they already have a good relationship with you, the preacher, they will give you the benefit of the doubt when you say something questionable. If the sermon is dull they will be prepared to wait longer to see if it livens up later. When other people in the congregation are enthusiastic and friendly, then your message is more likely to be well received.

Love

Sometimes your congregation just need to be loved into the kingdom. They are difficult, they're counter-suggestive, they're grumpy, they're their own worst enemies. Just like you and me in fact.

If preachers love their congregations and want the best for them it shows, and it persuades.

Respect

Do you respect your congregation? If you don't think they're very bright, and you can't be bothered to work hard on a sermon for them, then this will show, and you will fail to persuade.

Their emotions

Most people are not cold, calculating, rational beings. People are persuaded by their emotions far more than they realise. This is not something to be afraid of in church but it doesn't mean that we have to manipulate feelings and whip up false emotion.

It does mean that we should not be afraid to speak with passion about what we believe. If we are not passionate about our God, then we can hardly expect the people who listen to us to be convinced.

Their instincts

People intuitively know some things in life. They know that the world isn't the place it should be. They know that there is a difference between right and wrong. They know that Jesus Christ was an amazing man, and they would very much like to believe that he is so much more.

We can persuade people by appealing to their best instincts. The world spends its time appealing to people's worst instincts: What's in it for me? How do I gain?

Most people would like to live better lives than they do, and an appeal to their best instincts can persuade them to change.

Jesus did this when he said, 'The rulers of the Gentiles lord it over them . . . but you are not to be like that. Instead, the one who wants to become great among you must be your servant.' (Matthew 20)

He was reminding his disciples of something we all instinctively know, which is that true fulfilment comes in service to others, and that getting to the top of the pile isn't all it's cracked up to be.

Part of the preacher's powers of persuasion comes from reminding people of what they already know to be true.

Clarity

People are persuaded when you are clear. No matter how well-disposed they are towards you, if they don't know what you want them to do, then they're going to have a problem.

At the end of the sermon, there should be no doubts as to what it was about, and no doubts as to what the next step should be.

If your logic is confused in any part of the sermon, then this will make it harder for people to trust the rest.

You want to persuade them, so it is your job to be clear. It is not their job to listen so carefully as to be able to compensate for your inadequacies. You are not doing them a favour by letting them listen to your polished tones. They are doing you a favour, by being prepared to listen to you in the first place.

Make every effort to be clear.

Honesty and integrity

A truthful preacher is a great persuader.

If you tell people that Christianity is easy, and that you've never had a difficulty since you became a Christian, and life is a bowl of cherries, they are going to think, 'It's all right for you, chum, but my life is a mess. What have you got to say to me?'

Jesus had plenty to say about how it was the sick who needed a doctor and not the healthy, and how the Good News was for the poor. A sermon should be for those (like the preacher) whose life is not perfect, not for those who have everything worked out.

Preachers should be honest and talk about their doubts and fears, but how they are still prepared to trust God despite it all. If you find something difficult to understand, *then say so*. Don't say, 'I believe all suffering is God's will' if you don't believe it. Do say, 'We don't understand why there is suffering in the world, and heaven knows there's enough of it, but as Christians we believe that somehow Jesus Christ is in the midst of that suffering, and we are prepared to trust in him.'

Preachers should have integrity and not gloss over difficult questions and tricky parts of the Bible. If you tackle a problem head on, then people will be far more ready to listen than if you pretend it's not there.

Being honest means being true to the text and not twisting the sense. Being honest means being true to the congregation and not slipping things past them. Being honest means being true to yourself as a preacher and believing wholeheartedly what you are saying. (See the box about preaching other people's sermons.)

Being honest also means being polite about other religions. Just as voters are put off by negative campaigning against other parties, so congregations are put off by negative campaigning about other religions. Never say, 'Muslims believe . . .' unless you are absolutely sure you know what Muslims believe.

There are enough times when I hear on the radio or see on the television a church leader, who should know better, saying, 'Christians believe . . .', and I find myself shouting out, 'No, they don't! That's all wrong!' What they should be saying is '*Some* Christians believe . . .' If our church leaders fail to comprehend the diversity that exists within Christianity, what hope have we got of understanding the diversity that can be found in other religions?

Avoid negative campaigning.

Other people's sermons

Copying other people's sermons is very much frowned upon by the purists. This may have come from unfortunate incidents where preachers have gone on holiday and heard their own sermons preached back to them, but without the conviction that went into the writing.

I would say that for preachers starting out, other people's sermons are a great place to start. Very few bands start out by playing all their own material – most begin with cover versions.

Preaching somebody else's sermon will give you an idea of flow and structure that will help you learn.

Choose a sermon that speaks to you. If you don't agree with it, then don't preach it!

Then, rewrite the sermon in your own words and update it. You can use the same illustrations, but don't use them as if you were there (like the curate who copied sermons so often that he got lazy and began one Sunday by saying, 'When I was Bishop of Bombay').

Humility

People are attracted by humility in a preacher. At the end of the service you don't want people to say, 'You are a great preacher.' Instead you want them to say, 'We have a great God.' Your entire task is to point people away from yourself and towards Jesus Christ.

You must use the best of your intelligence and wit to craft a sermon that will make a difference, but you shouldn't let that cleverness show. In the same way that a party political broadcast is about getting votes, not Academy Awards, so your sermon is not about putting yourself above others. If you want people to know how clever you are, have your degree certificates framed and hung on the front door, so that people can see them when they come in.

The cultural references in your sermons should be ones that your congregation will recognise. You don't need to quote Plato and Aristotle to show how smart you are – although if they make the best illustration for your point, then use what they say.

In an essay it is important to make lots of quotations to show that you have read and understood the relevant material. A sermon is not an essay. When you use illustrations, let them show *others* in a good light rather than yourself. If there is to be a butt of a joke, let it be you. If there can be a twist in the tale, so much the better.

There is no place in the pulpit for snobbery of any kind: intellectual, musical, denominational, or class. You are no more than a beggar telling other beggars where to find food.

As President Kennedy might have said if he had talked much about preaching, 'Speak not about what you have done for God; speak about what God has done for you.'

An attractive presentation

The more attractive your presentation, the more likely people are to be persuaded.

The first thing you must do is to *entertain* the congregation. Now some people see this as 'dumbing down' and pandering to the lowest common denominator, but it isn't. To entertain literally means to 'hold the attention of'.

If you cannot hold people's attention, then they are not going to be persuaded. There is nothing wrong with being entertaining whilst you are trying to persuade. Honey catches more flies than vinegar.

You should use all the techniques available to hold people's attention. This can include humour, modern technology, visual aids, or whatever it takes. There are more details on keeping attention in

Chapter 6, and on modern technology in Chapter 11.

The key factor is that the content is still the most important thing. The presentation is not an end in itself, but a means to the end of persuading. If people come out saying, 'What a marvellous presentation', then you've failed.

A good worship experience

The best of sermons is going to flounder in a bad worship experience. But how can the rest of the service help you persuade people to vote for Jesus?

The important thing to remember is that the rest of the worship does not have to relate to the sermon, but it does have to be good. If there is a choice between a related hymn which is unsingable, or an unrelated hymn which the congregation will enjoy, then choose the one they can sing.

There is no virtue whatsoever in having an act of worship which is technically correct but cannot be understood. Use everything you can to help you in your task of persuasion. There are more details in *Cooking Up Worship,* the companion volume to this book. (See the resource section in Chapter 13.)

Lack of cynicism

I feel strongly about this issue, so please indulge me.

I find it particularly difficult when a man or woman of God will preach about the grace and love of God for this world, but then make a cynical remark. We are not here to say that 'all politicians are liars, only out for the money they can make for themselves'. That's not true, and if it was, we should be praying for them to change their ways, rather than having a cheap dig. *I* am persuaded by a preacher who thinks the best of others, and wants the best for others.

How long should a sermon be?

A sermon should be long enough to persuade, and no longer.

My guess is that because different traditions have different lengths of sermon, you are likely to be most persuasive keeping just below the time expected.

Thus if your congregation expects a five-minute homily, then to give anything more risks people turning off.

If your congregation are used to a half-hour sermon, they might regard five minutes as having been given short measure.

There is no set length for a sermon, and the result is the most important thing. Make your sermon long enough that people will vote for Jesus.

Personal testimony

People are ready to be persuaded by testimony providing that it is realistic and reasonable. If it is close to their own experience, then so much the better.

It is right for preachers to put themselves into their sermons. Phillips Brooks defines preaching as 'Truth through personality'. Your congregation can sit at home and read the lessons from the Bible just as well as they can hear them in church. The difference is what your personality brings to the preaching.

We are interested in the testimony of others and what it means for us.

Do you struggle with this text? Do you have questions about this issue? Have you experienced something like the person in the Bible lesson? Have you experienced something like I have?

If you are a man, and you are preaching about the experience of childbirth, I'll listen to you part of the way, but I would want the point of view of somebody who had actually given birth.

If you are preaching about suffering, or depression, or bereavement, I would expect you to have had *some* experience of it. That doesn't mean that you can't say anything until it's happened to you, but it does mean you should be careful in speaking of things which others have experienced and you haven't.

What is the difference between a sermon and a homily?

A homily is a short sermon.
A sermon is a long homily.

Relevance

People are persuaded when the sermon is relevant; when it 'scratches where they itch'.

If the sermon is about nothing that matters to them, then there's no point in changing their point of view. If the question being examined is 'Which of Paul's letters is the earliest?', then no matter how hard you might try to persuade people that the answer is Romans, then even if they do change their minds, so what?

Chapter 4 has direct advice about how to be relevant.

The Holy Spirit

I've saved the Holy Spirit until last, but, in one sense, it is only the Holy Spirit who can persuade. All our persuasive qualities cannot change people's hearts, but the Holy Spirit can change even the hardest hearts.

But the Holy Spirit is not a 'Factor X' that we add to our sermons at the last minute to make them work.

Instead, I believe that the Holy Spirit works *despite our sermons*. It is a miracle of grace that people can listen to the Gospel and respond at all. The preacher's job is not to make a sermon so good that the Spirit is happy to operate. Instead, the preacher's job is to get out of the way and to keep as low a profile as possible, so that the Spirit – not the preacher – can reach people's hearts.

It is when the preacher's profile is too high that the sermon gets in the way of the Spirit. When the preacher is arrogant, or dishonest, or unclear, or cynical, or irrelevant, then the Spirit tries to work but the congregation is too busy noticing the faults of the preacher.

When the preacher is ostentatiously intellectual, or uses rhetorical flourishes, or draws attention to his or her wit, then the Spirit tries to work but the congregation is too busy noticing the great qualities of the preacher.

When the preacher is humble and wants to persuade, then the Spirit can work, because the preacher will get out of the way.

May your sermons be all about God, and not about yourself.

Chapter 3

What shall I say?

I want to persuade; I'm ready to preach. What shall I preach?

One answer is to say along with St Paul, 'Preach Christ crucified', and there is a lot of truth in that. As Christian preachers, we're not persuading people to save the earth, be better educated or to be polite and kind to their neighbours, although that might be part of our message.

Our keystone, our central point, our unique principle, is that Jesus Christ is the Son of God and that he died and rose again. That should inform everything we say. To encourage somebody to vote for Jesus is not to get them to vote that they think Jesus was a nice man, or that they approve his manifesto. To vote for Jesus is to put your trust in him, and to want him to be your leader and to offer to do his will.

In order to get people to vote for Jesus we have to talk about him. Talking about Jesus necessarily means talking about his death and resurrection. That does not mean that every sermon we preach has to be directly about Good Friday, but that the events of Easter are the key to explaining the whole of Christianity.

There will be few party political broadcasts on any manifesto pledge that would not show a picture of the leader of the party somewhere in the programme. Preaching on any subject at all should show a picture of Jesus somewhere in the sermon.

Gospel truth

A second and similar answer is often heard: 'Preach the Gospel'. By this people usually mean that they want a 'salvation message': 'Don't preach to us about the way we should live our lives or the ministry of Jesus and his call upon us. Instead tell us how Jesus saves, how Jesus welcomes to himself all those who turn to him and how he offers forgiveness and new life. Give an invitation for those who want to become Christians to come to the front.'

Now I would argue strongly that this kind of preaching does have a place and that people should be offered the opportunity to vote for Jesus in this way, several times a year.

But I would also say that if the sermon each week is the same, then it starts to lose its effectiveness. If people are told each week, 'This could be your last chance ever to respond to the Word', then they are going to start ignoring it. If the same party political broadcast was scheduled week after week, viewers would switch off even more readily than they already do.

If the layman who preached when

Spurgeon heard him hadn't talked about salvation, then Spurgeon might never have been converted. On the other hand, if that layman had preached about salvation every week, then the chapel might have shut.

You can never know whether there will be a stranger in your midst on a Sunday who needs to hear the message for the first time. However, for most Christians, coming to faith is a longer-term process, and you want them to vote for Jesus this week and next week and all the weeks in the future, until it comes naturally.

So what subject should you preach upon?

As you preach Christ crucified, and as you preach the Gospel, you have the whole Bible from which to choose.

Preachers should always use the Bible as their basis, because that keeps us on God's agenda. A preacher is not a taxi-driver or a hairdresser. They are not there to give their personal opinions on the state of the world, but to give God's opinions.

We can find out God's opinion when we read our Bibles. The trouble is that the Bible doesn't always contain God's opinion on issues in today's world, and sometimes it isn't clear what God's opinion might be. The craft of the preacher is firstly to discern God's opinion, and secondly to persuade others to take that opinion themselves.

This means that preachers can take the same biblical passage and present sermons with differing views of God's

opinion, because they have discerned that opinion differently. Or each can take a different passage and each produce a sermon with a contradictory opinion.

Preaching from hymns

At a pinch you can use lines from a hymn as the basis of your sermon. Many of these lines come from the Bible anyway.

However, not all hymns are divinely inspired, so it is best to keep them for a 'talk' rather than for preaching.

Preaching about saints

Some traditions preach about saints.

It would be inappropriate to do this, unless you are using the story of the saint to persuade.

If you want to *inform* your congregation about the life story of a saint, then a lecture or a magazine article would be more appropriate.

Bible readings

The most straightforward way of producing a sermon is to pick a biblical passage, and then talk about it. If you need advice as to which passage to choose, then you can use a lectionary.

A lectionary is a list of Bible readings for each Sunday in the year.

Many lectionaries have been created over the years, but most Protestant Churches throughout the world have now standardised on the Revised Common Lectionary (RCL). This has been created by expert representatives of the churches to cover large amounts of the Bible and many themes. It matches very closely the Roman Catholic lectionary, and means that, throughout the English-speaking world and beyond, previously divided churches have the same set readings on a Sunday. For each Sunday there are three readings – one each from the Old Testament, the Gospels and the Epistles – and an appointed Psalm.

Why does the lectionary last three years?

Three is just an arbitrary number. There is no reason in theory why there shouldn't be a one- or a five- or a ten-year lectionary.

However, in practice three seems to be a good number in that we don't get the same readings every year, but neither do we only hear important passages once in a blue moon.

Year A is based on Matthew, Year B on Mark and Year C on Luke. Passages from John's Gospel appear throughout the three years.

The lectionary covers three years, so you shouldn't hear a duplicate sermon unless you happen to be in church the same Sunday three years later. Of course, it isn't as simple as that. Some readings appear several times in those three years and some passages never appear at all.

Helpfully, the team that put together the lectionary called the years Year A, Year B and Year C.

Unhelpfully, they started the lectionary with the liturgical year, rather than the calendar year. This means that

Year A, Year B and Year C all start on Advent Sunday and finish on the Sunday before Advent. (See 'Learn your ABCs'.)

Learn your ABCs

- Year A starts in December (or sometimes even late November) in 2001, 2004, 2007, 2010 and covers most of but not all 2002, 2005, 2008 and 2011 respectively.
- Year B starts in December (or sometimes late November) in 2002, 2005, 2008, 2011 and covers most of but not all 2003, 2006, 2009 and 2012 respectively.
- Year C starts in December (or sometimes late November) in 2003, 2006, 2009, 2012 and covers most of but not all 2004, 2007, 2010 and 2013 respectively.

This is all very confusing, and gives you plenty of opportunity to make mistakes and get the wrong year – not that many people will notice.

The advantages of using the lectionary:

- Themes are chosen which might not be included otherwise.
- More of the Bible is 'covered'.
- Books can be looked at sequentially over several weeks.
- You won't be repeating what last week's preacher said.
- You don't choose your pet subject every week.
- The passages chosen may well match those used by the Sunday School or Junior Church.

- We don't go through the cycle of the Church Year *because* we believe; we go through the readings year in and year out *until* we believe.
- There is a lot of help available in magazines, books and on the Internet (see the resources section, Chapter 13.)

My sermon has three points – it took me nine hours to rearrange it until it did, but I've finally done it!

The disadvantages of using the lectionary:

- There is a temptation for preachers to try and link together the three passages, rather than to make one persuasive argument. The readings are not necessarily designed to 'go together'.
- They are set by theologians, not ordinary people. The passages answer the questions that theologians are interested in, *not* necessarily the questions that ordinary people ask.
- You are looking at a theme that somebody else has picked.
- They tend to concentrate on some themes and not on others.

Bowdlerisation

Dr Thomas Bowdler (1754-1825) published versions of the Bible and Shakespeare without the bits that might be considered offensive.

The lectionary does the same. In Year C, the story of Elijah and the prophets of Baal is given as 1 Kings 18:20-21 (22-29) 30-39.

This tells the story of Elijah's God setting fire to the sacrifice, whilst the god Baal fails. The verses in brackets (22-29) are suggested for omission, as they describe Elijah mocking the other religion, and this is presumably not politically correct.

The story really ends at verse 40, when after defeating the prophets, Elijah slaughters all 450 of them. This is conveniently omitted from the lectionary version.

Like it or not, there are bits of the Bible that are considered offensive today, and it is the preacher's job to help explain them.

If one of your congregation is following in a pew Bible and you stop at verse 39, they will think that you have something to hide. Instead you should deal with verse 40 head on.

Christianity has nothing to hide – there is no secret knowledge. As Richard Nixon might have said, 'It's not the crime that takes you down – it's the cover-up.'

- If there are other factors at play, then using the lectionary can overburden the service. For instance if there is a baptism, or it is the church anniversary, or Racial Justice Sunday, it would be unwise to try to attempt to link in the lectionary theme. Instead, choose just one idea for the sermon, and mention the others in passing.

- The lectionary 'Bowdlerises' the Bible. (See 'Bowdlerisation', page 27.)

- You can only preach a sermon once every three years. It is good practice to take a particular sermon and refine it by preaching it several times in different churches. You can't do this if you follow the lectionary.

A more excellent way

In this book I want to argue for a different type of preaching altogether. I want to say that although lectionary preaching has its place, it is not sufficient in itself to persuade people to vote for Jesus. Preaching from the lectionary is only relevant by chance.

It is relevant to people's lives when the subject is something that impacts upon them. When we start from the Bible passages that the theologians have chosen, we are looking at issues that were important to people thousands of years ago, and may or may not be important to us today.

I suggest that we should start from where people are, and then bring the Bible to bear. I think we should look at what is important to people today, and then look at the Bible passages which speak about those issues.

In a sense the lectionary already does this, in that there is not a great deal of material from Leviticus and Numbers, as those books are seen as having less to say to us than Isaiah or Jeremiah. But I want to go further than the lectionary and create preaching which persuades people to vote for Jesus. I think this can only be done with sermons that are relevant to today. The next chapter explains how.

How to read the lectionary

The most difficult part is working out which year you are in. Once you have done that, you will find for each Sunday there are anything up to 12 readings.

The example we will take is for the Sunday in Year A between 2 and 8 October inclusive, also known as the 27th Sunday in Ordinary Time, or Proper 22. (All that means is that it's not a special Sunday like Advent or Easter.)

The readings are given as follows:

	Principal Service *Continuous*	Principal Service *Related*	Second Service
Old Testament	Exodus 20:1-4, 7-9, 12-20	Isaiah 5:1-7	Proverbs 2:1-11
Psalm	Psalm 19	Psalm 80:7-15	Psalm 136:1-9 (10-26)
Epistle	Philippians 3:4b-14	Philippians 3:4b-14	1 John 2:1-17
Gospel	Matthew 21:33-46	Matthew 21:33-46	Mark 10:2-16

The Principal Service is the main service on the Sunday, usually the morning. The Second Service is often the evening service.

For the Principal Service, churches can follow the *continuous* readings or the *related* readings. In both cases the Gospel and the Epistle are the same.

Because we are in Year A, we are going through Matthew's Gospel. Last week it was Matthew 21:23-32 and next week it will be Matthew 22:1-14. In the same way for the Epistle, last week it was Philippians 2:1-13 and next week it will be Philippians 4:1-9. A preacher taking all three Sundays (or working in a team) could follow through on the lessons.

The Gospel passage is the parable of the ungrateful tenants of a vineyard. Jesus is saying that Israel is God's vineyard. The Philippians passage is Paul talking about how Christ is more important to him than anything else.

In the Old Testament the *related* passage is Isaiah 5:1-7 which is also about a vineyard with ungrateful people in it. That vineyard is Israel. A straightforward sermon could be preached, using the passages from Isaiah and Matthew. The passage from Isaiah has been deliberately chosen to match up with the Gospel reading.

The *continuous* Old Testament reading is from Exodus, as is the previous week's and the week after's. The passage chosen is about the Ten Commandments, and has little relation to the Gospel reading (although you can make anything work if you try hard enough). You would only want to use the *continuous* reading if you were following through the Exodus passages over the weeks.

If you are using the Psalms in worship, and not everybody does, you will find that

→

the *related* Psalm 80:7-15 once again compares Israel to a vine. It has been deliberately chosen to match up with the readings from Isaiah and Matthew. The *continuous* Psalm 19 hasn't.

For those churches using the *related* readings, it would be appropriate to use one, two or three of the readings together.

For those churches using the *continuous* readings, you should choose either the Gospels, *or* the Epistles *or* the Old Testament readings and *use the same one every week*. The official advice from the creators of the *continuous* lectionary is that preaching should be 'sequential' rather than 'thematic', and you should not 'hop, skip and jump' around among the three sections of the Bible. In other words choose Matthew *or* Exodus *or* Philippians and stick with it.

As regards the second service, we are going through Mark's Gospel and the first letter of John in the evening. The Gospel passage is about marriage followed by the famous 'Suffer the little children to come unto me'. The Old Testament passage from Proverbs is about a parent teaching a child and is *related* rather than *continuous*.

Note also:

- The *continuous* Old Testament reading is Exodus 20:1-4, 7-9, 12-20, the Ten Commandments. The reason why they have done it this way is to keep all the commandments together and to make more 'sense' of them. If you want, you can read the whole passage, Exodus 20:1-20. It can be dangerous taking out verses, especially if we remove ones we don't like. See the box on 'Bowdlerisation' on page 27.

- The Second Service Psalm is 136:1-9 (10-26). The verses in brackets are optional and do not need to be included.

- The Principal Service Epistle is Philippians 3:4b-14. Chapters and verses didn't appear until over a thousand years after the Bible was written. Sometimes the people who decided where the verses should go got it wrong. The first half of verse 4, is actually the end of the sentence from verse 3. A new sentence starts half-way through verse 4, and that is the start of this reading. Philippians 3:4b means Philippians, Chapter 3, Verse 4, second half.

Chapter 4 _____

_____ Focus groups

You can preach the most wonderfully constructed sermon in the world, with the finest scholarship and most beautiful language, but if it is not relevant, it is not going to get people to vote for Jesus. One of the biggest criticisms that comes from the pews is that preachers are not talking about the world in which real people live. There's too much academic discussion of the world of the Bible, and not enough about the world of today.

Now after my sermon last week, Bob here is very excited to know, 'What happened to the Amorites and Jebusites next?'

But how can we make our sermons relevant? And relevant to whom?

Politicians find out what issues are relevant to the public by using opinion polls and focus groups.

In the Church we have had focus groups for years. We call them either Bible Studies or House Groups. They are excellent places to find out what questions people really have, and what issues are foremost in their minds. Good preachers always have their ears open, to hear the concerns of people.

Those preachers who are also pastors have an advantage. When they go visiting, they get to hear the joys and delights, and the fears and concerns of their flock. The questions that are raised become the basis of sermon material. So if you visit somebody who tells you that they are 'worried about their son who is living with his girlfriend, and they don't feel right about it, and he doesn't come to church any more but what can they do because they don't want to turn him away?', then that is the opportunity to work on a sermon about 'What do you do when your children won't come to church?' Because there will be other parents in exactly the same position wondering what they can do, and what the Church has to say.

Now there are various answers to this question. You could write a sermon condemning the practice of cohabitation. You could write a sermon saying that it doesn't really matter and that a wedding certificate is just a piece of paper so what's the fuss? Or you could write a comforting, encouraging sermon about how Christianity is not hereditary, how they can still love somebody without approving what they do, and that it's not necessarily their fault that their children have turned out this way, because you only have to look at the Old Testament kings where good fathers had bad children and bad fathers had good children, to see that producing the perfect son or daughter is not possible. Then you could give them practical advice and tell them that they can still pray for their children, that they can still bring their grandchildren to church, and that they should welcome strangers to the church, because they will be somebody else's child or grandchild. In a situation where it is difficult for people to see how they can vote for Jesus, you can show them.

How much guilt is taken away just by bringing the question into the open and talking about it?

The great preachers throughout history have had this knack of 'scratching where people itched'. They have been able to speak directly to the heart, because they have known their congregation's hearts. They have instinctively understood the issues which were relevant. In the same way, the great politicians have been able to strike the right note, because they have had the innate ability to know what voters were thinking.

For the rest of us who are not great preachers, and don't have this amazing intuitive empathy, we have to work at it. There is a good way to find out what is relevant to other people – ask them.

You can do this very simply, formally or informally, in groups or for individuals. If you can't get things done by intuition alone, use a recipe. (See 'Mama Large's biscuits'.)

The recipe I used was a one-page anonymous questionnaire which asked people:

- their age and gender
- whether they were a regular church-goer or not (yes, no or sort of)
- what three questions they would like answering from the pulpit

I took the questionnaire to a variety of churches, the local university where I am a chaplain, and to the local prison. The results that were gathered are reproduced here.

The questions people wanted answering were not all worded the same way, but I took 'How come if there's one God there's so many religions?' and 'Why would you believe that non-Christians, believers in other faiths, go to hell?' to be basically the same question, and put them with 'What about other religions?' along with various other variations on the theme.

Mama Large's biscuits

My wife's grandmother in Alabama used to make the most wonderful biscuits. She would take a 'bit' of flour and a 'bit' of sugar and 'just the right amount' of shortening and add a 'splash' of milk to make the dough, before putting the mixture in a 'medium' oven. She never used a measure, because she knew the way it should look.

The rest of the family did not inherit her intuition, so they use recipe books.

> ## Top seven questions over all (in order)
>
> - What about suffering?
> - What about other religions?
> - How/why did you become a Christian?
> - How is church relevant?
> - Do you have to go to church to be a Christian?
> - Prove that God exists.
> - What is the meaning of life?

There were lots of questions that were unique to the questioner, where just one person had an interest in a particular subject. Some of these appear in the 'interesting questions' box on page 39.

There did not seem to be any difference in questions by gender. There was

> ## Top seven questions of people who don't go to church
>
> - What about suffering?
> - What about other religions?
> - How/why did you become a Christian?
> - How is church relevant?
> - Do you have to go to church to be a Christian?
> - Was Jesus the Son of God or just a man?
> - Prove that God exists.

a difference in approach to the questions by age, in that many of the young (non-churchgoing) students at the university were stuck for an answer and had to be given time to think, whereas the older respondents were much more forthcoming. This may be because the younger people were not interested in 'religious' questions.

One issue that kept coming up time and again, however, and tops the list of each category of people I interviewed, is the problem of suffering.

Over to you

But the point is not that you use the lists on these pages as the basis for *your* sermons. These questions were relevant to some people in specific situations in Liverpool at the beginning of the twenty-first century.

Perhaps the problem of suffering would come near the top in every survey. But you need to find out what questions are relevant to the people to whom *you* will preach in *your* context.

The way you do this is to ask them what their questions are, in whatever way is easiest for you, whether it is a questionnaire, a group or some other way.

Bear in mind that sometimes people will tell you what they think you want to hear, so they might not be the real questions on their hearts. Consider also that it can take time for people to understand what you want of them. Basing your sermons on the issues relevant to people is a process, not a one-off exercise. If you start to inform your sermons by the questions people are asking, then they will be prepared to ask more questions. If they never hear their questions answered, then why should they bother doing the exercise again?

Top seven questions of people who *do* go to church

- What about suffering?

- How is church relevant?

- How/why did you become a Christian?

- What about other religions?

- How can I follow Jesus today?

- What is the meaning of life?

- How can we share our faith?

What do they think?

There is one difference between politicians and preachers. Preachers want to know which major issues are relevant in people's lives. Politicians want to know that, but they also want to know what people think about those major issues, and then they tailor their policies accordingly.

It is not your job to tailor God's policies to the views of your congregation. Your aim, in finding out what is relevant, is to be able to tell people about what God wants them to do on the big issues that concern them.

So, for instance, if you discover that crime is a big issue and that people are very worried about it, then it is right to

preach a sermon on it. However, if the people you talk to think that criminals should be 'strung up from the nearest lamp-post because that's the only language they understand', it doesn't mean that is what you should advocate from the pulpit.

Instead, you could talk about a Christian attitude to crime and criminals, and encourage people to do something about it, by becoming prison visitors, neighbourhood watch co-ordinators or volunteers for victim support. You could also talk about forgiveness, reconciliation, restitution, law and grace, or even tax evasion.

You could look at the New Testament and talk about the thief on the cross, or storing up treasures in heaven, or turning the other cheek (what might that mean in the context of the legal system?) or 'let the one who is without sin cast the first stone'. You could look at the

---

Top seven questions in prison

- What about suffering?

- Do you have to go to church to be a Christian?

- What am I doing here?

- Prove that God exists.

- Is there life after death?

- Was Jesus the Son of God or just a man?

- Has science disproved religion?

- How/why did you become a Christian?

Old Testament, where there are some terrible crimes committed, including rape, kidnap and murder.

The important thing is that you provide a Christian viewpoint on an issue which matters to people, rather than an academic viewpoint on the history of the Israelite nation.

Top seven questions in the university

- What about suffering?
- How is church relevant?
- What about other religions?
- How/why did you become a Christian?
- What is the meaning of life?
- Do you have to go to church to be a Christian?
- Why is God always 'he' and Jesus always white?

Seven questions Christians ought to be asking (in my opinion)

- What is the Christian attitude to money?
- What is the Christian attitude to sex?
- How can I love my neighbour?
- What does it mean to love the Lord your God with all your heart, soul, mind and strength?
- What is worship?
- How can the Church be more like the kingdom?
- How can I give up my power, like Jesus did?

What if people are asking the wrong questions?

Quite probably they are. There are lots of questions that people should be asking about the world in which we live. Maybe it is because they are complacent, or maybe it is because they don't understand that they cannot formulate these questions properly.

But if you patronise your congregation, or look down upon them because you think you know best, then you are unlikely to be able to persuade them to vote for Jesus.

It is time that we learnt to trust our congregations. We are not asking them, 'How should we think about an issue?', which is a question that can be debated.

We are asking them, 'What issues are important to you?', which is a question that has answers which are not to be argued over. If somebody tells us, 'I want to know about the issue of suffering', it is not for us to say, 'Oh no, you don't. You don't want to know about that at all. You want to know about this week's lectionary readings.'

We have to accept people where they are. It's no use complaining that they haven't got a working knowledge of the books of the Apocrypha. If they haven't, then they haven't. You will just have to manage without, and preach sermons that don't depend on your congregation being enlightened the way you think they should be.

You can come up with your own questions and that's fine. But be aware that although the questions may be relevant to you, they won't necessarily be relevant to the people to whom you preach. And remember that somewhere out there is a preacher who thinks it is important to know what *did* happen next to the Amorites and Jebusites.

God's agenda

There *is* an argument which says we should not be talking about our agenda, but about God's agenda. This thesis sees the Bible speaking to us directly and holding up a light to the way we live. Our lives and their lack of love are illuminated by the Bible until we see the way we should go. When we read the Bible in the community of the Church, we receive God's revelation of the way God wants us to live.

I don't think that my approach of using questions is incompatible with this. When we read the Bible in church, we can only read a very small part of it at a time. When the Bible readings come from the lectionary, they are the theologian's agenda, and the Church's agenda, which is not necessarily the same as 'God's agenda'. When the Bible readings are chosen according to the questions that have been raised, they are at least 'the people's agenda'. As such, the people are more likely to be receptive to the revelation of God's will, because they will be listening to something that matters to them.

We want people to vote for Jesus, and we need to give people reasons why they should do this. If one of those reasons is 'Because it really matters', then we are more likely to be successful.

What about consistency?

If a church is following the lectionary, then it gets a consistent message over a period of weeks. Theoretically. If you are answering different questions, then it won't. Does this matter?

No, it doesn't matter. It is vitally important that each individual sermon is consistent, and that there is no confusion in what is being said. But over time it does not matter whether the message is consistent. The Bible as a whole has a lot to say, but it doesn't always agree with itself. If you try to turn the Bible into a monochrome book that says one thing, you end up getting in knots. If you try to preach the same message over and over again, the congregation loses interest.

It is in the everyday working-out of the Christian life, in complicated situations, that the decision to vote for Jesus is made. Sometimes it is not at all clear what that vote should be. At other times, different Christians will give conflicting advice.

Most of your congregation will be used to living in an ambiguous world like that. On some issues we can state clearly in black and white what a vote for Jesus means. On others there are shades of grey.

It is perfectly acceptable to preach one week from Galatians, and talk about how we need nothing else but grace, and then the next week to speak about Matthew 25 and the sheep and the goats, and to talk about the need to do good works. To put them together in one sermon would be difficult. To have them on consecutive weeks as different aspects of how God relates to us and how we relate to God is fine.

The real danger of preaching over a long period of time is repeating yourself and being *too* consistent. There are only a limited number of sermons to go round. Whatever the text, some preachers have a habit of returning to a pet theme and doing it to death. One of the advantages of facing up to the questions that people are asking is that it forces you to look at different subjects.

How do you answer the question?

The standard sermon is the 'expository' sermon. The preacher goes through a Bible passage line by line and word by word, and explains what it means. This is a great way of leading a Bible study, but I don't think it is the best way of preaching.

Congregations regularly say that they want 'biblical preaching', but when they get real expository preaching they consider it too dull and academic. What I *think* they want is preaching that tells us what the Bible says about issues of today, rather than a verse by verse voyage through the Bible.

The contrast is between 'biblical preaching' and 'unbiblical preaching' – we want to know what the Bible says about this issue, rather than what some trendy Oxford theologian thinks. This may be a false contrast anyway.

I think the best way to give congregations what they want and need is to base the *structure* of your sermon on the question posed, and your *content* on relevant Bible passages. This is better than basing the structure of the sermon on the Bible passage, and the content on what the commentaries say about it.

It is often argued that starting from the Bible is *the* way to preach, because that is where we find God's word. But that's not the way Jesus preached.

There were times when he preached from the scriptures, such as when he opened the scroll at the prophet Isaiah in the synagogue (Luke 4). Yet most of the time Jesus preached by looking at the world around him, and commenting on what he saw based on his biblical knowledge. Jesus brought the words of the Old Testament to life as he used it to analyse the present. Jesus did not always preach *from* the scriptures, but he used the scriptures to look at contemporary issues.

Seven questions that were asked of Jesus

- Should we pay taxes to Caesar?

- Who is my neighbour?

- Who is the greatest in the kingdom of heaven?

- Is it lawful to heal on the Sabbath?

- How can a man be born when he is old?

- What shall we do with this woman caught in adultery?

- What is truth?

I think we should follow his example, and not always preach starting from the Bible. Instead we should start with the issues of today, and then use the Bible to analyse those issues.

Jesus was also asked questions – many times to trap him. He used the Bible in answering those questions.

Dialogue preaching

Rather than hearing one voice, it is possible to have two or more voices speaking. A *dialogue* is held where different points of view are represented and the argument goes forward and back.

In political terms this is a bit like a debate between the party leaders. However, in our situation where we want people to vote for Jesus, we have a particular view of which way they should cast their ballot. You can offer different alternatives, as long as they are both valid ways of voting for Jesus, and as long as it is not confusing.

Storytelling

A more modern approach (or maybe an older approach!) is the storytelling sermon.

Here, stories are told, and through the truths contained in these stories, enlightenment comes to the listeners. Congregations reach their own conclusions, which work on many levels. In one sense, Holy Communion can be seen as a visual kind of preaching, for there is a story, with meaning, that works on many levels.

Storytelling *can* be used to answer the questions that are being asked. It is a worthwhile way of preaching, but only if it persuades people of your point.

I don't mind a storytelling preacher, but I'm not having a karaoke one!

Topical preaching

On Tuesday, 11 September 2001, terrorists attacked America with hijacked aeroplanes. The Sunday afterwards, there could be only one subject.

On Sunday, 31 August 1997, Princess Diana was killed. On that morning there would have been no point preaching on the lectionary, or telling a story, or answering a question in which the congregation had expressed interest.

On those days, preachers had to change their sermons to try and put into context events of great significance.

By their very nature, these events cannot be predicted. Whether they are local, national or international events, it is the preacher's job to be ready to postpone the carefully prepared sermon, and to respond to the incident which is on everybody's mind.

Variety

If you are one of a number of preachers who go round a group of churches, then you do not have to provide variety. The styles, gifts and graces of the others will provide variety enough. Instead, concentrate on perfecting your own style – maybe this style of answering questions.

If you are preaching in the same place week in and week out, then you have to provide your own variety. I would suggest that there would be some weeks when this style of answering questions would provide a different approach. This would be useful in itself, but it would also reinforce the other kinds of preaching you do. By answering questions you are modelling a mature, questioning faith. When you return to expository or lectionary preaching on another Sunday, then it will come across as a different style again. If you preach from a text week after week, although the text will change, the style won't and that could be a problem.

Seven questions I thought were interesting

- Where would Jesus be on Sunday, and with whom?

- God forgives me. How can I forgive myself?

- How can you focus on prayer?

- Why is human flesh being punished for crimes committed entirely through the influence of the devil?

- Why should people give you authority to speak on these matters?

- If you go to heaven and a loved one goes to hell, then how could you be happy in heaven?

- What are we doing when we worship in church?

Why do a questionnaire? Why not let people bring their questions with them?

The whole point of doing the exercise is to find out the questions people want answering. An anonymous questionnaire allows them to ask whatever they like, and gives you time to prepare a well-thought-out answer.

If the sermon becomes a question time, then some people will not ask what is on their hearts, other people will ask questions to show how clever they are, and you will have no time to formulate effective answers.

A question time may encourage people to vote for the preacher, as a witty person who can debate cleverly, but it won't necessarily help them to vote for Jesus.

Suffering

The clear winner in all the categories of people questioned is the issue of suffering, which comes with many variations.

It may be that you need to do a whole series of sermons on the question of suffering. It is unlikely that you will be able to 'crack it' in one address, so you could take different aspects of the question each time.

You could preach on:

- Why is there pain in the world?

- Why do some people suffer and not others?

- Does God punish people with suffering?

- If God can stop suffering, why is it allowed to continue?

- Did God want Jesus to suffer, and, if so, why?

- Are the sins of the fathers visited on the children?

- Would we choose a world with no pain, but no free choice?

There are a large number of Bible texts that you could use. The book of Job in the Old Testament is all about the problem of suffering. In the New Testament you would want to look at the letters of Paul, and in particular at the death and resurrection of Jesus. There are several really helpful books on the whole issue of suffering that you could be reading in order to inform your answers.

They told me they only understood the real meaning of suffering after they heard me preach.

You are not going to come up with 'an answer' to the problem of suffering, but you can help the people in your congregation to start to come to terms with this issue through your preaching.

A more excellent way

I hope that I've convinced you to take seriously the questions that people have.

There are times when it is appropriate to preach from the lectionary, and to follow the seasons of the Christian Church, but there are also times when it is right to answer the questions that people are asking, and to which they are finding no answers. Even worse, they may be finding answers in all the wrong places, and thinking that the Church has nothing to say.

By answering the questions that people are asking, you can help them to vote for Jesus.

Maybe I have persuaded you to go so far as to be ready to answer one of the questions in your next sermon. How do you go about it?

I would argue that you should base your entire sermon on the question. You should outline the issues, look at potential answers to the question, and then choose one or more of them which you advocate. Then you should give straightforward, practical advice about what your congregation should do next.

The next three chapters look at the end, middle and start of such a sermon, beginning with the question of where the sermon should fit in the worship.

Seven questions I thought were unusual

- Where is Elvis?

- Am I going to resit my exams?

- How can I make a million pounds?

- Why do people always like doing the things worst for them?

- Is greed brought about by advertising?

- Do you believe in God or do you believe in yourself?

- Why was God going to kill Moses until Ziporrah circumcised his son? (Exodus 4:25)

Chapter 5

The ending

If you are going to persuade people to see their lives changed, then you have to give yourself the best possible opportunity of doing so. That means putting your sermon in the best slot in the service. That place is at the end. The words of the sermon should be ringing in people's ears as they leave the church. Nothing should come after the sermon which does not reinforce its persuasive powers.

An obvious way to finish is with the sermon, followed by a hymn which powerfully hits home the message, and finally a blessing and dismissal, as the congregation are sent out to 'vote for Jesus'. (Other alternatives are discussed later in this chapter.)

If you have another part of the service *after* the sermon, then by the time you get to the end of the service people have forgotten it.

A classic three-fold approach to worship is 'Approach – Word – Response'. Most worship services can be categorised in this way.

We *approach* God with praise and confession, bringing our prayers, our cares, our sins and our joys.

Then we hear the *Word*, read and preached.

Then we make our *response*.

In recent years there has been a trend to move the sermon further forward in the worship. We listen to the sermon, and then we make our response by saying more prayers. I believe very strongly that the sermon should be at the end of the worship. We *approach* God in the same way, and we hear the *Word* in the same way, but we make our *response* after we walk out of the church door. It is in the world that we need to respond, not in the church. It is Monday to Saturday that we need to vote for Jesus, not just on Sunday.

If you are preaching on Luke 10, the parable of the good Samaritan, the required response comes in verse 37: 'Go and do likewise.' The right response is for the congregation to go out and be good neighbours. The easy response is for the congregation to pray that other people will go out and be good neighbours.

Don't get me wrong, prayer is essential, but it is not the only response that should be made to a sermon.

In James 2:17 we read, 'Faith by itself, if not accompanied by actions, is dead.' I believe that a sermon by itself, if not accompanied by actions, is dead.

A party political broadcast finishes with a striking call for you to vote for the party, and an address to write to for more information if you want to become a member. It does not finish with anything else, because the most important thing is for you to cast your vote.

The sermon should send you on your way into the world with a striking call for you to vote for Jesus. Anything that follows it must be in direct support of that aim.

Coming to a conclusion

When you construct a sermon, the first part to think about is the ending. How are you going to finish? What are you trying to persuade people to do?

You should be able to state the aim of your sermon in one sentence. If you can't, then the people hearing it won't be able to. By the end of your sermon, everyone who has been listening should know exactly what you would like them to do.

The sermon shouldn't just drift to a close. There must be a clear, straightforward, obvious ending. Nobody should look up and think to themselves, 'Hang on – is it over?' (See 'Song'.)

Try to avoid saying 'and finally' or 'in conclusion' more than once. To let people know you really have finished, say, 'Amen.'

Your sentences should start getting shorter as you reach the end. You should be able to see the shape of a triangle in your manuscript (assuming that you're using one). The sermon should also slow down. The more slowly you speak, the more important each individual word becomes. It will also help your congregation to concentrate. It doesn't have to be melodramatic, but it should grab their attention. (See the box on the right.)

Song

Some songs are designed to be faded out – the main theme is repeated endlessly until the sound dwindles away. A good example of that is 'Hey Jude' by the Beatles. Your sermon should not end like that.

Other songs have a definite ending. The music comes to a close and you can tell it is about to finish as it slows down with a slight variation on the theme. A good example is 'She loves you' by the Beatles.

Your congregation should be able to hear your sermon coming to a close about a minute before it does.

Your final words should be the most persuasive. You can have a good start, where the congregation is prepared to be swayed by what you have to say, but by the time you get to the end, you may have argued yourself out of contention. People may have been ready to cast a ballot for your idea earlier on, but now you have to clinch their vote.

You are also after repeat votes in that you want people to vote for Jesus again and again and again over the years.

The end of a sermon on Mark 1:17

(Come follow me and I will make you fishers of people.)

Simon and Andrew were called by Jesus, 'Come, follow me.'

In the same way today, Jesus calls us, 'Come, follow me.'

To each person here, Jesus says, 'Come, follow me.'

To *you*, Jesus says, 'Come, follow me.'

Are *you* listening to Him?

'Come, follow me.'

'*Come.*'

Amen.

This is not the place for emotional blackmail and telling people that this is their last chance because they might be dead tomorrow. The statement is technically correct, but many people don't respond well to being bullied in this way.

How often, in electrical appliance showrooms, do we see the 'deal of the century' on a washing machine, but only if you pay cash today? If you walk away and come back tomorrow with cash, then the same deal has miraculously been resurrected. A good rule-of-thumb in life is this: If you want an answer today, the answer is 'no' because if a deal is not available tomorrow, then it's usually not a very good deal.

However, as Christians we don't want people to delay and dither about casting their vote. How can we encourage them to make a decision? The answer is by being honest. (See the box on the left.)

You need to know in advance what you want people to do. You want them to vote for Jesus. How can they cast that vote?

In Chapter 1 we looked at several different ways of casting a vote for Jesus. For each sermon, before you begin writing, you need to think what you would like people to do. Once you have decided what you would like to persuade people to do, then you can start writing.

Let us use our example sermon from Mark 1:17. To vote for Jesus in this context means deciding to follow him. What might it mean to 'Come, follow Jesus'?

Ideally there should be a range of responses on offer, rather than a take-it-or-leave-it deal. In your congregation there will be a variety of people. There will be those who have been Christians for years. There will be those who are new Christians. There will be those who are nearly Christians. There will be those who are agnostic. You may even have atheists in the congregation. People go to church for all kinds of reasons!

Your sermon is a 'one-size-fits-all' outfit. It would be wonderful to be able to tailor the message for every individual listening, but that is not possible. Fortunately, as Christians we believe that the Holy Spirit can take our message and enable people to really hear it. Sometimes they hear more than we bargained for. (See 'What did I say?').

The bit just before the end of a sermon on Mark 1:17

(Come follow me and I will make you fishers of people.)

Now I know you'd react badly if I told you that this could be your last chance to follow the call of Jesus. You'd be thinking it was emotional blackmail if I said to you that you had to decide today because next week you might be dead. You're going to be here next week to listen to my next sermon, you lucky, lucky people.

But there are times in your life when you do have to make a decision. At some time in your life you do have to get off the fence. You can't sit there for ever. You won't be dead next week, or so we hope, but I can assure you, if there's anything I've said today that's true it's this: 'You're not going to keep going for ever.'

'Unlike this sermon,' I can see you thinking.

Simon and Andrew could have asked for more time but they were ready to follow. What's holding *you* back?

What did I say?

Many preachers have had the experience where a member of the congregation has said, 'Thank you for your message, that was just for me. It really hit home when you talked about the need for forgiveness.'

After they have walked away, the preacher wonders where that came from, because it certainly wasn't in the sermon that had just been delivered.

However, you *can* offer people different ways to respond positively when they hear the words 'Come, follow me'.

For those who are not yet Christians, the call is clear to make a commitment. For those who are already Christians but have issues in their life which need addressing, then the call is to face those issues and do what they know to be the right thing. For those who are Christians but feel their faith has gone dead, then the call is to recommitment. For those who are Christians but feel restless, the call is for new commitment to a new area of service. For those who are Christians and are feeling quite complacent and happy, then the call is to ask God to show them where they can go forward. (See the box on the right.)

Every sermon should have some elements within it which are applicable to:

• established Christians

• new Christians

• those who are not yet Christians

It is no use just preaching to the converted. Nor is it any good assuming that nobody in your congregation has

The bit before the bit just before the end of a sermon on Mark 1:17

(Come follow me and I will make you fishers of people.)

So what is Jesus calling *you* to do? What does it mean for *you* to be his follower today?

I don't know. I can't say. I don't know how his call is working on *your* heart.

But if you're not a Christian, then his call is to follow him by becoming one. He wants you to be one of his disciples, not because you are good or clever or whatever. The only measure he uses is that you are willing.

If you are already a Christian, then his call might be to new areas of service. Jesus could be calling you to a new level of commitment. If you know what you are being called to, then have a word with me afterwards. If you *don't know* what you are being called to, then have a word with me afterwards and I might have some suggestions.

If you used to have lots of faith but now you feel a bit battered, then maybe his call is to recommitment. If you have issues in your life that need addressing, maybe you need to recommit yourself to the way that in your heart of hearts you know to be right.

And if you don't fit into any of these categories and you're feeling sad that you've been missed out – or, alternatively, you're feeling rather glad that you've been missed out, then maybe Jesus' call to you is a wake-up call for you to listen. Maybe you should be praying that God will help you to hear the call that is being made.

Jesus calls us as individuals. How are you going to respond?

ever heard of Jesus before. You might think they act as if they have never heard of him, but that doesn't mean that they haven't. Try to use language that all kinds of people will be able to understand. (See Chapter 8.)

After the sermon is over – what are you going to do next?

It would be a complete anticlimax to preach the sermon above and to finish with 'Come, follow me. *Come*. Amen. We'll now sing hymn number 999, "All things bright and beautiful".' At the very least there should be a slight pause after the 'Amen', to allow the words to sink in. Even better if the hymn was directly related, such as 'Will you come and follow me if I but call your name?'

But there are other options. Remember your aim is to get people to vote for Jesus. In this case you want them to respond to his call and to follow him. What could you do to maximise the impact of your sermon?

Come down to the front

This traditional response gives people the opportunity to do something physically to show their commitment. Coming down to the front of the church is visible to everybody else so it can be difficult for shy people. It is appropriate for preachers to kneel at the rail so that they are responding to the call too.

If an appeal is made rarely, it becomes a very big deal, which some people might find intimidating. Even worse, the people upon whom you wanted to make a big impact might be away that week and miss their opportunity.

If an appeal is made every week, your congregation can start to get fed up with hearing the same thing each time.

One potential solution is used by many churches in America. Each week the communion rail is 'open' for those who want to come down and respond to the message whatever it is, or just to pray. If a congregation can get used to the practice, then anybody who wants to come down the front to make their own prayers can do so, and it isn't quite so unusual for the rest.

Ask the rest of the congregation to stay in an attitude of prayer whilst people come forward.

Variations on the theme which make it easier for shy people are for everybody to put their heads down in prayer, and then those who want to make a commitment should put their hands up, or lift their eyes, so that you as the preacher can see their response, but nobody else can.

Follow-up is essential afterwards. (See 'Who tames the bear?')

More worship if you must

A time of silence or of prayer after the sermon gives people a chance to think about what you have said. But if you want to make a longer-term impact, it would be even better if you could get them to have a time of prayer every day.

Responses can be made physically, with symbolic acts of penitence or intercession.

In some circumstances there will be communion after the sermon. To maintain the impact of what you've said, remind them of your words as you call

---

Who tames the bear?

A pastor and an evangelist are out bear-hunting when they stop for lunch and put their guns down.

Suddenly, out of nowhere, a ten-foot grizzly bear appears and starts chasing them.

Without their guns, they're no match for the bear, so their only hope is to get to the cabin.

They sprint as fast as they can with the bear after them. The evangelist gets to the cabin first, opens the door, and the pastor runs in, closely followed by the grizzly bear, after which the evangelist slams the door shut, but stays outside.

'What are you doing?' is the pastor's desperate cry from inside.

'I'm an evangelist – I just get them in. Once they're in, it's the pastor's job to sort them out.'

---

them down to the table. If you are calling for some kind of commitment, invite people to make that commitment as they receive the elements.

After the event

If calling for an immediate response is not appropriate, then there can be other follow-up options.

Don't hide the ballot-box! Make it easy for your congregation to vote for Jesus by having prepared ways in which they can respond.

If you've called them to vote for Jesus by reading their Bibles every day, then take enough Bible-reading notes with you to hand out at the end.

You could put together a follow-up pack with everything necessary in it. So

if you want people to vote for Jesus by writing to their MP and protesting about Third World Debt, then put together a postcard pack so that all they have to do is write their name and address.

Best of all would be for there to be a group which meets to follow up all the ideas that have come out of the sermon.

You could give out sermon notes (or even a full transcript) for people to read later. If there was something you wanted people to remember, then you could give them a card to stick on the fridge (Jesus is calling me to something new), which would remind them every time they went for some milk. A well-known variation of this is the 'WWJD' wristband, which reminds the wearer to ask, 'What would Jesus do?'

You could be calling for volunteers to take food to the homeless, after your sermon on the need to follow the words of Jesus in Matthew 25. They could see you after the service, or meet on Monday night at the church, or they could sign up for duty in the foyer.

You could have a 'commitment form' available, with a whole lot of different options which people can sign up for. This can be in the pews, or handed to people on the way out. (For a more creative alternative, see 'Under the pews' on page 48.)

Always think ahead to your plans for after the sermon. You should be ready with everything needed to help people act in the way you have asked them to.

Remember, you want them to vote for Jesus this time, but to keep on voting for Jesus again and again and again. A bad experience today might stop them from doing so.

Under the pews

'Now I want you to look under your seat right now, because there's somebody here today whom God is calling to a special commitment, and there's a commitment form under their seat.

Keep looking under your seat to see if it's you.

My word – it's amazing! You've all got one! I guess that must mean that God has a call for everybody. . .'

One more question?

For those who are brave, there is one more suggestion for after the sermon.

A friend of mine who is a minister asked his youth club what they thought of Sunday services. They said that they could take the hymns, and the prayers, and the readings, and the things that they found dull, as long as when the sermon was over, they could ask questions.

And why not? Questions allow the congregation to clarify points and to understand what you really meant if it wasn't comprehensible the first time. It also allows them to raise objections and counter-examples. These might be very easy for you to rebut, which would strengthen your case.

Be assured that just because counter-examples are not usually shouted out at the end of a sermon, it doesn't mean that people aren't thinking them.

The only problem I found with this system when I tried it was that the services went on too long. Once the questions started, and the debate began, it was hard to bring it to a close. Some people liked it, and it showed what pent-up desire there is in our congregations to grapple with real issues, but other people didn't like it as the length of the services grew.

Why not give it a try next time you preach? It helps to have a 'plant' to ask the first question so as to break the ice. You should announce at the beginning of the sermon that there will be questions afterwards.

Be on your toes, and look out for the 'clock-watchers'.

This was Lee's fifth follow-up question . . .

Chapter 6

The middle

The central part of the sermon is where you try to answer the question that has been asked. Sometimes that question has a straightforward easy answer. Sometimes it doesn't. But that shouldn't stop you from giving some kind of answer.

Always tell the truth. You can answer a question by saying, 'Well, I don't know the answer, but I would say . . .'. You can be clear in saying that an issue is complex, rather than speaking obscurely about what can be known.

It is quite acceptable to say, 'The issue of following Jesus is complex. What does it really mean to follow Jesus? Can it really mean that we follow him to the cross?'

It is not right to say, 'I'm not sure whether there's anywhere in the Bible where Jesus would ask us to follow him even unto death.' You should be sure – it's in Matthew, Mark and Luke – all you have to do is look.

Some of the best sermons come from honest wrestling with the issues. Christianity has nothing to hide. There are no questions that you're not allowed to ask in case the whole thing will collapse. Instead, a sermon should look at difficult issues which are close to the bone, even if the answers are hard too.

As Christians, we can't always say to somebody, 'I know how you feel.' But Jesus can. Because Jesus had the same struggles that we have today, we have a friend who can sympathise with us in all our weaknesses. Your congregation will find it easier to appreciate a preacher who has the same struggles, rather than someone who finds life easy.

In order to persuade people to vote for Jesus, you have to tackle the issues that matter, issues which are sometimes very difficult. But you still have to be clear, so that people can understand what you've said.

One point turn

The best way to be clear is to have one point. Traditionally sermons have three points. (See the box below.)

In the previous chapter I claimed that you should be able to sum up your sermon in one sentence. If you have one point, it should be easy to do. If you have three points, it is going to be harder.

World, Church, individual

One preacher was noted for taking every text the same way. He would give a three-point sermon on 'What does this text mean for the world, for the Church, and for the individual?'

When he wanted variety in his preaching, he would ask, 'What does this text mean for the individual, for the Church and for the world?'

Remember, the aim of the sermon should be 'short and pithy', not a paragraph long!

In the example from the previous chapter, using Mark 1:17 (Come follow me and I will make you fishers of people), the aim is simple but profound: to get people to come and follow Jesus.

There are at least three *applications* at the end of the sermon as to how different kinds of people should follow Jesus. But there is one aim – to get people to follow Jesus. And there is one point – Jesus is calling you to follow him.

Rather than making three separate points, try to make that one point over and over again. There are many ways of voting for Jesus, but today, at this time, you want to persuade people to follow Jesus.

In the text, Simon and Andrew are being called to follow Jesus in order to become *fishers of people*. Now this is true, and this is valid, and this is interesting, but it is for another sermon. There are lots of important points to be made about becoming fishers of people, but they are for another Sunday. No matter how tempted you feel to include some great material on this topic – save it. It will come in useful another day.

For today, be content to be persuading people just to follow Jesus, as that is your aim. If you want to talk about fishers of people, restate your aim, and plan your sermon again from scratch.

Outline

One way of persuading people to follow the call of Jesus is to show how he has called people throughout history.

He called Simon and Andrew, and you can talk about that. He called famous Christians, and you can talk about them. He called Christians whose names we don't even know, but we can see the effect of their work in the way the Church is here today 2000 years later.

Once you have shown that Jesus has called a large number of people to follow him in the past, you can tell them that he calls people to follow him in the present. He called you to be a preacher, and you can talk about your call.

Then you need to tell the congregation that Jesus is calling them.

Try to think of any objections they might have and state them out loud. 'But I'm not good enough,' I hear you say. Then answer the objection. Jesus calls all kinds of people, good and bad in the eyes of the world, including Simon and Andrew, who didn't do such a good job later in the story.

'I haven't heard the call of Jesus,' I hear you say. Well, you're hearing it now. Jesus calls people in all kinds of ways, including through the words of the preacher, so you've no excuse.

'It's too difficult,' I hear you say. Well, not many things in life are easy. Much is expected of those to whom much has been given. The challenge is there.

If you can think of any more objections to quell, so much the better.

Let everything you talk about support the main point that Jesus is calling people in your congregation to follow him.

How can I keep the attention of the congregation for the whole sermon?

I don't think you can, so don't try.

You have to be a great preacher to be able to do that. Some of the great names of the past could do it. Dr Sangster could apparently preach for an hour, and people thought that it was just a few minutes.

But for ordinary preachers like me, it is too lofty an ambition. Instead, we have to accept that we are not going to keep the attention of our congregations all the way through, so we must work out a different strategy.

The real question we need to answer is, 'Once we have lost someone's attention, how can we get it back?'

There are techniques we can use to help those who have drifted off to come back. These include

- the pause
- the thump
- the whisper
- the joke
- the question
- the unfinished sentence
- the repetitive phrase

If you *pause* for more than the very shortest moment, people will look up from their slumbers to see what is happening. The longer the pause, the more time they have to refocus.

The classic way of gaining attention is to *thump* the pulpit. A good sharp hit, especially if there is a microphone attached, can raise the most somnolent congregation.

You can only thump so many times before it starts getting annoying. A different option is to vary the quality of your voice by *whispering*. This isn't a quiet whisper, but a stage whisper. People only whisper when they have something important to say, so your congregation will strain to hear.

Humour is a great way of keeping a congregation's attention and grabbing it again. If they think that at any time you might tell a really funny *joke* then they will listen more carefully. If they have already drifted off, then the laughter of those around them will reconnect them to the task in hand.

The *question* which requires an answer means that people have to speak, and speaking brings us back to listening again. These are not rhetorical questions where the preacher is expecting no answer. These are real questions to which there is a simple answer that you hope will be given. For instance, 'We're now ready to move to the next part of the sermon. Are you ready for the next part of the sermon?' Silence.

'We'll try that again: are you ready for the next part of the sermon?' 'Yes.'

Once again your congregation can reconnect. It doesn't have to be quite so blatant as that, but any question that requires people to respond gives you the opportunity to bring them back to your theme.

A similar technique to the question is the *unfinished sentence* which requires completion. 'You'll remember that in John's Gospel, Jesus said "I am the resurrection and the . . ."' At the same time use your hands to gesture that you are asking a question. You should get the response 'life'. As people respond, it brings them back to the content of your sermon, but also reinforces the message.

Middle bit of a sermon on Mark 1:17 when the congregation need to re-enter

(Come follow me and I will make you fishers of people.)

Which brings me to one of the most interesting but also most unimportant questions in scripture. Are you ready for an interesting but unimportant question?

When Jesus called Simon, Andrew, James and John, had he met them before?

And people say, 'Well, he must have met them before, even though it doesn't mention it, and he must have been well known to them, and they must have followed him because he'd already taught them a lot.'

And when you press further and ask, 'Why do you say that?', they respond, 'Well, it stands to reason. I wouldn't just drop everything and follow Jesus immediately. They must have known him before.'

But the point is you wouldn't drop everything and follow Jesus if he called you immediately, or if he gave you a three-year intensive study course on being a disciple. It's completely irrelevant how long Simon and Andrew and James and John knew Jesus; the important part is that they *followed* him, whether having been called for

→

---

the first time, or after a long time.

If I asked you today to come back to my house with me in my car and said, 'I will make you fishers of people', I bet you wouldn't fancy it. If I spent a year offering you intensive training, and then asked you to follow me, you still wouldn't fancy it.

The amazing thing is not that those disciples went after Jesus *immediately*, but that they went after him *at all*.

Now we've looked at one of the most interesting but also most unimportant questions in scripture, are you ready to get back to the main topic: 'What does it mean to be a follower of Jesus today?' You are? Good.

This is even more powerful if you use your main theme as the unfinished sentence. 'Jesus is calling you to . . .'. If you receive the response 'follow him', then you are hitting home.

This underlines the value of the *repetitive phrase*. If you can include the key sentence at the end of each segment of the sermon – 'Jesus is calling you to follow him' – and follow it with a short pause, then people can reconnect and know that a new point is coming.

In diagrammatic form many sermons look like this:

$$A \Rightarrow B \Rightarrow C \Rightarrow D \Rightarrow E \Rightarrow F$$

The problem is that this logical progression is fine for an essay, where you can go back and read again what you didn't understand. But in a sermon, if you are not paying attention when point C is explained, then points D, E and F don't make any sense because they depend on a vital part of the argument that you've missed.

A more successful form looks like this.

$$\text{B} \quad \text{C} \quad \text{D} \quad \text{E} \quad \text{F}$$
$$\text{A} \nearrow \searrow \text{A} \nearrow \searrow \text{A} \nearrow \searrow \text{A} \nearrow \searrow \text{A} \nearrow \searrow \text{A}$$

Point A is the main point which is repeated throughout. If any of points B to F are missed, then the argument still stands. Ideally everyone in the congregation should be with you all the way through. In the real world this doesn't happen, but in the second diagram the main point is not lost.

A classic example of this technique can be found in the 'I have a dream' speech by Revd Dr Martin Luther King.

What about two-part sermons then?

Instead of having one 20-minute sermon, you can have two 10-minute sermons, split by a hymn, or a prayer or a sketch.

This does allow for re-engagement for those who have let their minds drift away. It can work, as long as it is not an excuse for two separate sermons on different points. If you think it can help people to vote for Jesus, then do it.

How deep can my sermon be, whilst remaining clear?

It can be as deep as you like.

Depth and clarity are not opposites.

The opposite of deep is shallow or trite. The opposite of clear is vague or ambiguous.

A sermon can have both depth and clarity. Unfortunately sermons can also be both vague and trite.

A useful tool for helping us here is 'Jardin's Principle'. Jardin says that any issue can be looked at in three ways: simplistic, complex and simple but profound.

For instance, a school can assess its performance in these three ways. In a simplistic way, it can say, 'We need to raise standards.' In a complex way it can produce a full curriculum and work out the best use of support staff to make an 'integrated learning experience' (whatever that might be). In a simple but profound way, the school can say, 'We need to provide an environment in which children can learn.'

The final answer raises a whole new set of questions. What kind of environment do children learn in? How can we help children learn? How can we affect the environment out of school so that the children are ready to learn when they come in? And many more.

When we look at the life of Jesus, we see someone who is neither simplistic nor over-complicated in his approach, but who is simple yet profound.

Take Luke, Chapter 20, the issue of paying taxes to Caesar. The original question is 'Is it right to pay taxes to Caesar or not?'

Now a simplistic answer at this point is either 'Yes' or 'No', and, either way, the Pharisees have got him. If he says, 'Yes', then he might just as well be a collaborator with the Romans in the eyes of the Jews, who hated paying the taxes, and abhorred the coins with Caesar's head on them. If Jesus says, 'No', then they can tell the Romans that he is a tax rebel, and even if they won't intervene in religious disputes, they will definitely sort out anybody who is a tax dodger. In fact three chapters later on, the chief priests and teachers of the law bring him before Pilate, and unjustly accuse Jesus of opposing taxes to Caesar.

But Jesus says neither 'Yes' nor 'No'. Instead, Jesus asks, 'Whose head is on the coin and whose inscription?' To which the answer comes: 'Caesar's.'

A complex answer at this point would be to say, 'Ideally taxes should be used for the benefit of the local population and there should be political representation, and a progressive income-based direct formulation, plus a low cost of collection and proportionate penalties for those who renege on their responsibilities.'

Instead, Jesus said, 'Then give unto Caesar that which is Caesar's and unto God that which belongs to God.'

This is both simple and profound. It's simple in that it can easily be understood, but it's profound in that it raises a whole new set of questions. What does belong to Caesar? What belongs to God? How do we decide?

The job of a preacher is not to give simplistic answers, nor to give over-complex academic answers suitable for an essay at theological college. The job of the preacher is to be simple yet profound, to have clarity *and* depth, without dodging the issues.

So how can I be simple yet profound?

Your use of language is vital in this respect and there is more about this in Chapter 8. In particular, technical words should be avoided as much as possible.

You also need to speak directly to your congregation. Don't patronise them with 'There's a difficult bit here which I'm sure most of you won't understand.' You desperately want them to understand, in order that you can persuade them of your case. Don't try to impress them. They will be impressed by clarity rather than long words anyway.

Work hard to get your message across using the most straightforward words you can. Study and toil to cut down your manuscript and to remove all the bits that are clever, but which don't support the main point. See the box.

Maid in England

There is an apocryphal story of an eighteenth-century evangelical preacher who would practise his sermon on the maid. If she didn't understand he would get very frustrated, but go away and rewrite his sermon until she did. When she understood, he knew that the people he preached to in the street would understand.

Don't be afraid to raise further questions. If you are looking at the issue of poverty, remember that some of the greatest minds in history have looked at the problem, and have not come up with 'the' answer. It's all very well for your congregation to ask, 'Why is there poverty in the world?' What they should really be asking is 'How can we do something about that poverty?' You can tell them that the World Bank and economists have many complex theories as to why some countries have more resources than others, but that somewhere, somehow, it must have something to do with human greed. And when we talk about human greed, are we talking about other people, or must we include ourselves? Is poverty God's fault, or is it a direct consequence of human nature?

By raising more questions, you are not giving simplistic answers to the congregation, but allowing them to consider what the answers might be.

Just as the radio can paint more vivid pictures than the television because it works on your imagination, so a sermon which raises more questions calls upon the imaginations of the congregation, taking them further.

Don't be afraid of questions. As you are answering them, and asking them, you are modelling a mature faith which isn't afraid to hold up to the light some of the ambiguities of life.

That doesn't, of course, mean that you are ambiguous in your approach – far from it. But it does mean that you are not afraid of difficult questions, and that your faith is not afraid of challenge.

While you produce this middle part of your sermon, it might help to have written out your aim, and have it at eye-level, so that it can be constantly in mind. Once you have written out the middle, edit it down ruthlessly, and remove any part which doesn't support your aim of getting the congregation to vote for Jesus.

Chapter 7

The beginning

If the ending is the most important, the start of your sermon is the second most important part. You need to get the attention of your congregation in such a way that they want to listen. Then, once their concentration wanders, they will be happy to tune back in again.

The way to do this is to put your best material at the front. It's no use lulling them into a false sense of boredom before unleashing your brilliant ideas at the end. The congregation will have been lost long before. Instead, you have to start so well that they will want to listen more in case there is anything else quite so good on offer. Don't disappoint them!

Holy Spirit to come

There's the old story about the minister who had been called out over Saturday night to the hospital to see one of her congregation.

'I'm terribly sorry,' she announced on the Sunday morning, 'but unfortunately I haven't had any time to write a sermon, so I'm just going to have to depend on the Holy Spirit. But don't worry, it'll be a lot better next week when I'll be back in charge again.'

The very first thing to do is to say a prayer. This is for two reasons. One is to dedicate the sermon to God. You want God to speak through you, so it's only right to ask.

Some preachers use the words of Psalm 19: 'May the words of my mouth and the meditation of my heart be acceptable in your sight, my strength and my redeemer.'

Others use a formula such as 'Father, may my words be your words, and may your words reach deep into our hearts, in the name of the living Word, Jesus Christ our Lord. Amen.'

This shows your humility too, in that you want God to speak to the people.

The second reason for saying a prayer is to mark that the sermon is about to begin. If you use the same prayer each time, it becomes almost like a signature tune. People know that the sermon is coming up.

Sometimes preachers just launch into their sermon and catch the congregation on the hop. This lessens your chance of gaining attention, because nobody is sure whether you are making an aside, or commenting on the hymn we're about to sing.

A clear, well sign-posted start helps everyone to know what's happening.

Fifteen love

You've said your prayer, and now the congregation are looking up at you

56

expectantly (or at least awake), and there's that silence known to preachers, which is like in tennis when the ball is thrown up for the serve. It hangs in the air for what seems like an age, and then the rally begins . . .

What comes next is your opening gambit, and there are various options:

- the joke
- the explanation
- the story
- the context
- the quotation
- the text
- the question

The joke

The joke comes naturally to some of us. There are preachers who would make excellent stand-up comedians. They could tell a joke in the pulpit, on stage, at a party or wherever they had the chance. They make the joke, they get the laugh, and they move on with an attentive congregation. If they don't get the laugh, they have the comic's confidence to be able to make a comment about the congregation's failure to respond. 'I can see that it's a difficult crowd in this morning. I hope you're better than the lot I preached to last week. It was like treading the boards at the Glasgow Empire – if they liked you, they let you live.'

If you are a preacher who isn't very good at jokes, *don't tell jokes*. A sermon doesn't have to be funny. We can admire preachers who have the congregation laughing and smiling, and wish that we

were like that. But God has called us as well, and God has called us as we are, not so that we can be like other preachers.

If you tell a joke and it goes flat, and you're not the kind of person who can dig yourself out of trouble, then the whole sermon is likely to come across badly. If you don't do jokes, then choose a different opening.

The next question is 'Which jokes should I tell and how many?'

Everything in our sermon is subordinate to our aim of persuading people to vote for Jesus. We are trying to show people how great God is, not how funny we are. So the jokes have to be subordinate to the aim, too.

If there is any part of a joke which is in questionable taste, it has to go, no matter how funny. If there is any part of a joke which is offensive, then you are going to lose votes, so don't tell it.

Desert island survivor

A man was shipwrecked on a desert island for ten years before he was found.

His rescuers were very impressed to discover that he had constructed four large buildings in the time that he'd been alone.

He showed them round and explained that the building on the left was his house, and the building on the right was his workshop where he did all his construction, Monday to Saturday.

The building in the middle was his church where he worshipped every Sunday.

'But what about the large building over there?' asked one of the rescuers.

'Oh, that's the church I used to go to.'

If the joke is directly relevant then begin with it and follow the theme. The Desert Island joke would be perfect for a sermon on unity within the church.

If the joke is not relevant, but you want to grasp the attention of the congregation, don't try to make it relevant by forcing the details, or by making tenuous links. Instead, say, 'This evening's subject is "What does it mean to follow Jesus today?" which means I won't be able to tell you the one about the man on the desert island – OK then I will, but just this once.' And then tell the joke. Now there could be the vaguest link between the joke and the subject, but the time you'll spend bending everything into place would be better used in other ways.

Humour can be a great way of speaking to a congregation. In days of yore, the court jester was the only one who could tell the king the truth. Everybody else was afraid of what the king might do, but the court jester could sail close to the wind and get away with it, through his wit.

Another name for the court jester is the fool, and some of us can be very effective fools for Christ, using humour. We can tell people things about themselves using humour that we could never say directly. (See 'Pillars'.)

Try to laugh *with* people, rather than *at* people. And remember you can be humorous without telling jokes.

Don't tell too many jokes; otherwise there can be a danger of trivialising or belittling a serious theme.

Pillars

Contrast this:

'There are people here today who are blocks to the growth of this church, and they need to either shape-up or ship-out. The ones who are keeping the church open are the ones who are keeping it empty.'

With this:

'It's good to see our folk here today as usual, and it's good to know that the regulars, the ones we call the 'pillars of the church', are here. Do you know why we call them the 'pillars of the church'? Because no matter how hard you push them, they'll never budge!'

We all recognise this kind of person and smile, although, of course, it is always somebody else, never me . . .

The explanation

The explanation is a variation on the line, 'A funny thing happened to me on the way to the church this morning.' An explanation is different from a joke because it's not necessarily funny.

People are interested in how we come up with subjects for sermons. It can make a sermon far more powerful and engaging if we have a real-life situation which leads to our subject. For instance, 'My car was broken into on Monday when it was parked at the hospital. It's been on my mind all week, so today, I thought I'd speak about that.'

Lots of us have had our cars broken into over the years, and we are very interested as to what a Christian response might be. We know that we're supposed to forgive, but there's anger, a weary stoicism, frustration, guilt at having parked it in the wrong place, and a whole load of emotions with which to deal. We'd like to hear a preacher tell us how she coped with it, and how we can vote for Jesus, when we'd rather have immediate and harsh divine retribution on the culprits.

That has far more power than starting with the line, 'We live in a fast changing society in which some people experience social exclusion, which as a community we need to tackle.'

The story

In one way an explanation is a particular kind of story.

A story is wider than an explanation, because it need not be about yourself, and it isn't the reason why you are preaching on this subject. The story will engage the congregation and lead them into the subject.

A good example, and particularly relevant to all-age worship, would be the children's story *The Runaway Bunny* by Margaret Wise Brown. In this story, a little bunny tries to run away, but every place he decides to go, his mother is always there, because she loves him so much.

That would be a great way to start a sermon about God coming to seek us while we are still a long way off.

Of course the story doesn't have to be one that has been published, or one that is designed for children. It can be a made-up story or a true story, and it can be aimed directly at the adults.

> ## Text messages
>
> It has been said, 'A text, without a context, is a pretext.' But preaching the context of a text is a lecture.
> The sermon is not a lecture. Avoid.

The context

'When Mark was writing those words from our gospel reading, he was probably in Rome. Many scholars date his work at between AD 50 and AD 80. Most academics believe it was the first gospel to be written, and was designed for Gentile Christians. Matthew and Luke both had access to Mark when they wrote their gospels.'

The *only* possible reason you would start a sermon like this would be if you were seeking to persuade the congregation that Mark came before Matthew.

You should be ready to study the origins of Mark's gospel, and you can do this on your own or in a group. The Church can delve into the technical aspects of the Griesbach Hypothesis (Matthew was written before Mark) and its comparative strengths and weaknesses, but in a lecture or Bible study, *not in a sermon.*

Party political broadcasts don't begin with information about who printed the first manifesto and when. Neither should you.

If it's not going to persuade people to vote for Jesus, then cut it out.

> ## The seven least inspiring ways to start a sermon
>
> - My text today is . . .
> - The doctrine of partial atonement has always fascinated me . . .
> - I looked in the dictionary for the definition of the word 'propitiate' . . .
> - The Greek word σκυβαλα literally means . . .
> - In these slides of my time in the Holy Land . . .
> - St Augustine of Hippo was once asked . . .
> - When I was Bishop of Bombay . . .

> ## Poetry corner
>
> The words of a poem can look good on paper, but often are lost in a sermon. If they are really good words, your congregation may want to read them again.
>
> Why not print them out as a handout for people to take with them?

The quotation

A short quotation can engage interest. Even if it's from somebody famous, do say what they are famous for. If you quote Michelangelo, there may be many who think that he's a teenage mutant ninja turtle – and they'd be right – as well as those who think of him as a painter of the High Renaissance.

You are setting the tone for the rest of the sermon. To persuade people to vote for Jesus, you don't want to exclude them by making them feel small. This is not an argument for 'dumbing down'. If you are going to quote Aristotle or Plato, then do so, but provide some explanation of who they were, and what the quotation means, to make it accessible to all. The same is true of poetry. (See 'Poetry corner'.)

If you must quote in a foreign language, then do provide a translation.

The text

A specialised form of the quotation is a word from the Bible: the text. This is *the* traditional method of beginning a sermon.

The preacher announces her text, reads it once or twice and then begins. This can be particularly useful if you really are sticking to the text.

You could do a sermon on the text 'I am the way and the truth and the life' with sections on the four important words *I, way, truth, life*. You would then define, analyse and investigate each of the four words and make points along the way. The sermon would stick very closely to the wording and structure of the text.

Sometimes the preacher wants to talk about a completely different subject, but still feels that a text is necessary. This can confuse the preacher slightly, and if the preacher is jumbled a little, you can be sure that the congregation is jumbled a lot.

If a text will act as your memorable phrase (see Chapter 6), then all well and good, but if it doesn't, use your memorable phrase instead.

> ### Start of a sermon on Mark 1:17
>
> (Come follow me and I will make you fishers of people.)
>
> Today's question is, 'What does it mean to be a follower of Jesus today?' (Repeat)
>
> Some of you have asked this question in the survey we did. Others have asked related questions such as, 'How can I live like Jesus today?', but I'm going to concentrate on 'What does it mean to be a follower of Jesus today?'
>
> We will be using our Bible reading from Mark's Gospel, where Jesus called Simon and Andrew.

The question

It will come as no surprise that I want to suggest that the best way to start the sermon is with the question you are looking at.

This can be done explicitly so that the question is part of the structure, which further strengthens its impact.

Now, so far this is a straightforward sermon. You've set out the question, you've repeated it three times to establish it, and you will be repeating it again later on. You have said which Bible passage you will be looking at, and you are now ready to go.

This is the time to make your impact. If you put your best material first, the congregation will be paying attention and looking for another bit, just as good. If you start off dull and lead them into a false sense of mediocrity, with a view to a triumphant surprise ending, it's not going to work.

A sermon should not be like an Agatha Christie murder-mystery: total confusion to start with, but ending with a triumphant tying-together of all loose ends. You really need to hit home early on, whether it is with a joke, a story, an illustration, a personal example or whatever.

> ### The bit just after the start of a sermon on Mark 1:17
>
> (Come follow me and I will make you fishers of people.)
>
> Now my guess is that some of you are thinking that this question doesn't matter. Who cares what it means to be a follower of Jesus today? Why would anybody want to be a follower of Jesus today? Where would you find followers of Jesus today?
>
> If Jesus came to this city today looking for followers, where do you think he would go to find them? The churches? The schools? The universities? Well, you'd be wrong. When Jesus looked for followers in Galilee, he went down the docks and found some fishermen.
>
> Many people feel that Jesus only calls clever people, or experienced people, or talented people, but Jesus calls who Jesus wants, and if Jesus wants you, who are you to say he is wrong?
>
> So, if you say to me that you're not the right kind of person to follow Jesus, and you haven't got the right credentials to serve in the kingdom of God, then join the club with Simon, Andrew. James and John. They weren't the right people either. *But they did follow when they were called.*

Chapter 8

What language shall I borrow?

When we speak about God we are reaching the limits of language and the limits of logic. Whatever we try to say is limited by our human understanding. Yet we do want to say things about God, and on behalf of God. So what can we say?

What was the sermon about tonight, dear? It was about fifteen minutes . . .

The first thing to say is that we must use the language of everyday life. Church is not a place where we should do things differently, and Sunday is not a day when we should use different words from those we use Monday to Saturday. If we are to persuade, then we need to persuade with words that can be understood.

Every organisation produces its own jargon, and the Church has too. But in our search for votes we should never assume that the people in the pew know the hidden words and what they mean.

Taboo™

There is a board game called Taboo, where you have to describe a word given to you on a card, without mentioning five other related words.

Try a variation on this in your next sermon. You are allowed to use the words God, Jesus and the Holy Spirit, but you are *not* allowed to use the words:

- Salvation
- Redemption
- Justification
- Sanctification
- Religion
- Incarnation
- Theological

That doesn't mean you are not allowed to preach on these subjects – they are important. But you should be able to preach on these subjects *without* using these words.

So in an essay you might write, 'The author of the Johannine material presents Jesus as saying, "I am the way and the truth and the life."' In a sermon you would put, 'In John's Gospel, Jesus said, "I am the way and the truth and the life."'

Not only do we want the subject matter of our sermons to be relevant, we want the language of our sermons to be relevant.

Party political broadcasts use the language of the voters, and very often portray ordinary voters saying why they think the party is so good. They do not talk about the PSBR and LIBOR and the debt to spending ratio, because that doesn't win votes. They do talk about low interest rates on mortgages and full employment, because that *does* win votes.

You can use the language of the everyday to describe eternity just as well as you can use the language of the Victorian Church.

If you want a style to copy, then the short stories of Ernest Hemingway are regarded as being models of brevity. He uses simple verbs and nouns to sparing effect, to describe scenes precisely.

You can use long, academic, complicated words, provided they will help you to persuade your congregation to vote for Jesus. When you show how clever you are with words, some people may be persuaded that voting for Jesus is only for those who are clever. If you must show the congregation how smart and literate you are, find some other way of doing it well away from the Sunday service. Don't swallow the dictionary.

The use of long words rather than short words to describe a subject is the sign of a lazy writer, not a good writer. May your sermons be good, not lazy.

Definitions

When you are using the classic method of taking a text (see Chapter 7), then one of the ways to handle this is to investigate the meaning of each individual word. So if your text was John 15, and you were looking at the text 'Abide with me', then you might do some research on the word *abide*. You could then say, 'I looked up the meaning of the word *abide* in my dictionary, and there are in fact at least three meanings. Let me take each one in turn . . .' I suspect that many sermons have progressed in that manner.

This is all very well, but John's Gospel doesn't actually use the word *abide*. Because it was written in Greek, it says μεινατε which can be translated as 'abide' or sometimes 'remain'. It is the second person plural aorist imperative of the verb μενω. Does your congregation really need to know this?

If you are a Greek scholar, then you might be able to bring out some added meaning through your study. Otherwise you are talking about the English translation, not the original Greek. There are many differences in the meaning of words, and it is even more complicated in the Old Testament with Hebrew.

Scholars are not united in their translations of words. There is great debate about how we should read certain passages. Commentaries frequently disagree with one another. If you use a commentary to tell you the meaning of the Greek, then you run the risk of preaching the commentator, not the Bible.

If you must use a commentary, read it *after* you have written the sermon to counter any glaring mistakes, rather than before you have written the sermon.

In a Bible study, you would certainly want to look at the Greek behind the translation of the verse we read. In a sermon, I'm not sure how much more persuasive it would be to discuss the original. What is important is that you do not put too much weight on an individual word in English. (See a *certain* box on this page.)

Certainty

The preacher took as her text part of the story of the Good Samaritan in the Authorised Version, Luke 10:33: 'But a certain Samaritan, as he journeyed . . .'

'Note carefully,' she said, 'that this man was a *certain* Samaritan. He knew what he believed. He was sure, he was determined, he was *certain*. Not like the mealy-mouthed leaders we have in the Church today – he was convinced of the truth. We must be *certain* like him!'

Meaning

You also have to be careful with your use of language, because some words have different meanings in a religious context.

An example is the word *myth*. Outside academic theology, a myth is something that isn't true. For instance: 'It's a complete myth that only special people with years of training can lead worship.'

Theologians and biblical scholars have another use for the word myth as a 'story with meaning'. For instance: 'The creation myth in Genesis tells us truths about the nature of humanity.'

If you state that the creation story in Genesis is a myth, then most of your congregation will understand it the normal way, rather than in the way of academic theologians. Now, that might be what you want to say, but if it isn't, then use the language of every day, rather than the language of the church academy. (See the box below.)

Real world meaning	Word	Church meaning
A great song which can be sung by anybody and will live for ever	Anthem	A song which can only be sung by a choir, and goes on for ever
Being sorry for something	Apologetic	Defence of the truth of Christianity
Pertaining to the Church of Rome	Catholic	Universal
Attractive and gifted	Charismatic	Hand-waving
The widest range of cultures, black and white, male and female, young and old	Diversity	Slightly different liturgies for communion
Any item of expenditure greater than £10,000	Expensive	Any item of expenditure greater than £10
Usual, normal, regular	Orthodox	Men with beards dressed in black

Appearance

This is not just the clothes you wear (there is more about that in Chapter 9). Instead, you whole demeanour will communicate to your congregation.

Speak with more than words. If you preach that the Gospel is the most important thing in the world to us here at St Widget's, then any visitors would expect a well-maintained gilded palace rather than a falling down shack. If you preach that 'joy is abounding in your heart', then do it with a happy face.

That doesn't mean that you have to sport a fixed grin throughout. You are trying to persuade people, so let nothing of the way you look and act confuse the issue.

To an established Christian, who has an idea what God is like, it matters less how you come across. To a visitor or an immature Christian, the way you are can personify the Gospel. If you are snippy, precise, fussy and legalistic, you give the impression of that kind of God. According to the way you behave, God may come across as cynical, remote, uncaring and intellectual, or loving, thoughtful and kind. As a preacher you model the way God is. This is one of the reasons why it is good to tackle difficult questions in the pulpit, because if you take questions seriously, you are allowing a questioning, mature faith, and encouraging people to grow.

At first this can seem daunting. After all, how can you as an imperfect human being personify God? Don't worry, you don't have to be all seeing, all knowledgeable and all powerful. But you do have to love the people. Maybe not as God does, but with a love that wants the best for them.

People can tell whether you love them, and are persuaded by it. You must show this not only in your words, but in your whole approach and your body language. If you can show that you love them practically at other times besides Sunday, then so much the better. One of the advantages that ministers have over visiting preachers is that they have the opportunity to love their people Monday to Saturday, which gives them the authority to persuade on a Sunday.

Pastoral preaching versus hit-and-run preaching

The advantages of pastoral preaching, where you know the congregation well:

- You know the questions they are asking.
- You have the relationship which can help you be more persuasive.
- You have the 'come-back' later on, should there be any points that need clarification.

The advantages of hit-and-run preaching, where you will not be back again:

- You can tell home-truths without it being personally directed, on the basis that if the cap fits, then wear it.
- Just as it is sometimes easier to confess all your life to a complete stranger, so it is sometimes easier to respond to somebody new.
- There is no 'come-back' later on, should there be any controversial points.

Controversy

How controversial you are usually depends on how close to the knuckle you go.

The gospel is *offensive*, and people are sometimes going to be upset at what you say. The Good News for the poor, which turns the world upside down, can often leave the complacent feeling hurt and angry. That was certainly the experience of Jesus. In Luke 6, Jesus warns us: 'Cursed are you when all people speak well of you, because that is exactly what their ancestors did of the false prophets.' If everybody speaks well of your sermons, then maybe you're not doing it properly.

If you know you are going to be controversial, then don't be afraid to say so. 'This next bit is controversial, so I hope you're going to listen carefully to exactly what I say' is a great way of gaining the congregation's attention. They are wondering what is going to come next. Be very clear and leave your congregation in no doubt as to what you are trying to say to them.

Having said all this, there is a difference between preaching the truth and being gratuitously offensive. If you make an off-hand remark, you can put off the congregation who were otherwise quite happy to be persuaded of your point.

If you were preaching about 'What happens when we die', a throwaway disparaging remark about Frank Sinatra is completely unnecessary. It would be wrong because it was irrelevant and impolite, but most of all because it might stop you from persuading one person about your main point. Rest assured, the President of the Frank Sinatra fan club *will* be in your congregation that week.

Anything which hinders your powers of persuasion should not be in your sermon.

How do I know when I'm being controversial?

There are times when you think you have preached a straightforward, down-the-line sermon, when somebody attacks you at the end of the service.

This can be for several reasons:

- For something you didn't say. This is the flip-side of the unfounded praise which preachers sometimes receive, when a person says, 'Your comment about such and such helped me so much today', when you never mentioned the subject. You just have to grin and bear it.

Omnipotence?

The Sunday School teacher finished her lesson. 'So, class, you can see that Jesus can do anything.'

'Please, Miss,' said a voice from the back. 'I know one thing he can't do.'

'What can Jesus not do?'

'He can't please everybody, Miss'.

- For something you did say which you meant. If the criticism is for something in the Bible, then you can defend yourself by pointing out that the complaint is not against you, but against Jesus, and if they don't like what he said, then they should take it up with him and not with you.

- For something you did say which you didn't mean. If you made a throwaway remark that hurt somebody, then you should apologise first of all, and then learn from the incident so that it doesn't happen again. This member of the congregation is someone you want to influence and persuade for good, and today you have failed.

- For doctrinal heresy. This has varied over the years. It used to be that preaching 'salvation by works' or 'predestination' or the 'lack of divinity of Christ' would land you in hot water. These days you are most likely to be savaged by the tabloids and made to recant in public if you preach that Santa Claus doesn't exist.

- For your insensitivity. If you are preaching about suffering, and you say that God solves all our problems if we pray, then there will be some in your congregation who have prayed and prayed and prayed only to see a loved one die. They might want to take you to task. That doesn't mean that you shouldn't tackle a text such as John 14: 'Whatever you ask in my name will be given unto you.' However, it does mean that you are going to have to examine the question, 'Why are our prayers sometimes not answered?' with a little more awareness of how other people might feel.

- For your style. This is harder to take. Your 'style' of preaching will depend on your personality. If your style is criticised, then that is, in effect, an attack on your personality. Unfortunately, there will be some people who don't like the way you preach. You may be too serious, too flippant, too edgy, too solid, or too something. You can't win them all.

- For the reason that their daughter is ill and they are worried about her. Sometimes people are just angry at God, and you are God's representative on earth at this moment in this place. God is not doing what God should be doing and you need to have an explanation why. You can have been preaching about 'Manna in the wilderness' but they want to know why their prayers have not been answered. You may have said nothing wrong at all, but you just happen to be there.

In all cases be gracious and listen carefully. They may be right. You will be a better preacher if you can learn from your mistakes. Nobody gets it right all the time, every time. The great preachers still fail – but they are great because they keep on learning.

When the preacher would hit a nerve, Richard the sound-man would jam the sermon with well-timed feedback.

Heckling

You wouldn't normally expect to be heckled in a church context but sometimes you can be. If you are preaching in the street (see Chapter 9), then there's a very good chance you will be.

Once again be gracious in your attitude, as you are modelling the gospel. Try not to be snippy in reply. You are not a stand-up comedian, so you don't have to prove your wit if somebody says something, or walks out. There are a hundred-and-one reasons why somebody might walk out during your sermon (try starting by saying, 'I wonder how many of you forgot to switch the gas off this morning'). It is not necessarily a personal insult to you.

Similarly, people sometimes shout out at inappropriate places in the sermon or the prayers. Often this is nothing personal to you.

They could even want to ask a question, but not have the social conditioning to know that the preacher has traditionally been above contradiction or question. A gracious answer helps everybody, even if it is only that you'll be happy to tackle questions once the service is over.

Chapter 9

How to speak in public

You need a lot of energy and enthusiasm to be a preacher. Speaking in public requires much more physical effort than conversational speech. Everything must be much larger – the voice, the gestures and the personality.

What we have to say is so important and vital that we need to do what it takes to get it across. There is *no* virtue in a fantastic sermon that nobody can hear.

There are three things that go together to make an effective message. These are *audibility, clarity* and *oomph.*

Audibility is about volume and projection – making a loud enough noise, and sending that sound to the congregation. There are techniques which you can use to improve this.

Clarity is about diction and dialect – words not being slurred, and all the letters being pronounced. How many times do we hear of Jesus Chrise or the Holy Spirid? Dialect doesn't matter as long as your message is clear, well modulated and well produced.

Oomph will be discussed later.

Methods

There are different methods involved in speaking with and without a microphone. Unfortunately, there is no substitute for experience, and no easy way of gaining that experience without standing up and speaking in front of a crowd.

One good tip is to practise by going into an empty room (preferably the place where you are going to speak, although this is not always possible) and getting

---

What should I wear?

You should wear whatever will help people to be persuaded.

If wearing a red nose was the answer to people hearing my message, then I'd wear the biggest one possible!

Usually, it is not about making yourself more conspicuous but less. People don't need much of an excuse not to listen to your message. If you wear something outlandish, they will be thinking about your clothes, not about what you say.

Different churches have their own 'uniforms' which they expect preachers to wear. Let your clothes be unexceptional so that they blend into the background.

It's perfectly true that there are too many people in church who are old fuddy-duddies who shouldn't place so much emphasis on what the preacher wears. But while they do think that, you will have to meet them where they are and dress smartly, because it is more important than your freedom that they vote for Jesus too.

somebody to listen to you and make comments. Even then, an empty room is very different from a room with a crowd of expectant listeners.

Speaking in public is different from speaking in private. If you speak normally, then it will be too quiet for everybody else, and too fast, especially if you are nervous. If your public speaking sounds slow and loud to you, then it should sound about right to your listeners.

When you are using a microphone, don't forget to step back or to turn it off during the singing, or you will drown out everybody.

Look your audience in the eye. Don't stare off into space. Open your mouth wide. Stand up straight. Shoulders back. Keep your head up. And smile rather than frown!

A good book to read for advice on both audibility and clarity is *Your Voice and How to Use It* by Cicely Berry. (See the resources section in Chapter 13.)

The first two factors are technical issues, but the third and most important factor, *oomph*, is all about energy and the personality of the preacher. God can use any personality, but you've got to have one to start with.

There are seven ways to give extra oomph to your sermon. These are pitch, pace, pause, volume, tone, movement and emphasis.

Perfect pitch

The *pitch* of a sentence will vary according to its mood or its intention. A serious sentence will have a lower tone (deeper voice), a happy statement will have a higher tone (higher voice). If the intention is to ask a question, then the tone will rise at the end of a sentence.

The two sentences:

'This is the Word of the Lord' (even tone) would do well after John 3:16.

'This is the Word of the Lord' (questioning rising tone) might suit Psalm 137:9.

If you use a monotone (the same pitch throughout), then your congregation will find it hard going.

Pace needs to be varied too. Horse racing commentators get faster and faster as they reach the climax of the race. The horses are actually running more slowly as they run out of breath! The excitement is generated by the frenetic commentary as the finishing post is approached! There is no harm being excited by your subject as long as you don't go too fast for clarity!

Alternatively, the more slowly you speak, the more importance each word is given. You can slow down and speak more quietly to increase the effect of the sentence. So:

'Who is the answer to our sins?' (crescendo)

'There . . . is . . . only . . . one . . . answer. And that answer is . . . . . . Jesus Christ.' (whisper)

That last phrase also includes our next item, the *pause*. By pausing, you can give yourself the chance to breathe, your congregation the opportunity to refocus, and added emphasis to your words.

Volume has to be more carefully used. If you have a microphone, your changes in volume can be made extreme. It is alleged that a famous politician once annotated a speech 'weak point – speak more loudly', although that does sound apocryphal to me. Instead, I would say that you don't need to shout, but the whisper, the soft tone and the loud tone can all be used effectively.

Tone is to do with the shape of the face. If you are smiling then your voice will take on a different tone to when you are frowning.

You don't need to have a fixed grin. Instead your emotions should show in your face and in your tone. (See the box.)

Face up to it

(This story is attributed to Spurgeon.)

A tutor at a theological college told his students, 'When you speak of the delights of heaven, your body should talk as well. You should light up with the joy of what is to come. Your eyes should sparkle, your smile broaden, and your whole face tell of the glory of God. When you talk of hell, your ordinary face will do.'

Movement can be a matter of personal taste. You should put your whole body into preaching, which means using your arms as you speak. Hopefully your gestures are helping to get your points across, rather than being regarded as annoying mannerisms. Ask a friend to watch you preach, and then accept their feedback.

If you do walk about, the tip is to speak when you stop. Thus, speak . . . move to a different place . . . speak again . . . move back . . . speak once more. Don't talk on the move. Always face the front when you are speaking so that your lips can be seen.

Emphasis is about changing the weight on each word. The sentence 'I am the way, the truth and the life' can be emphasised in several ways. '*I* am the way' is different from 'I am *the* way' is different from 'I am the *way*'.

If your sentences have no variation in emphasis, then your listeners will not know what is important to you. In a party political broadcast, the emphasis points are more than clear. 'In the last *two years*, the rate of *unemployment* has **fallen** by *15 per cent.*' The message they want to get across is 'two years unemployment fallen 15 per cent'. The emphasis gets that message home.

Now is the winter of our discontent

The addition of oomph is not about turning you into an actor. Don't try to be somebody different from who you are. Speaking in church is not an opportunity to 'ham it up' and to put on a 'preaching voice'.

Everything is subordinate to your desire to encourage the congregation to vote for Jesus. In the same way that a football team has to establish their physical presence before they can start passing the ball about, so you have to establish your vocal presence before you can start hitting those points home. You cannot speak and demand an audience. You have to earn the right to be listened to, and you earn that right by speaking well.

The more effort you put into being heard, and into keeping the attention of the congregation, the more impact you will have. After a while it will become automatic and you won't have to think about it so often.

Politicians spend thousands of pounds on image consultants to make them come across better. You don't have to spend the money, but you should always be looking for ways to communicate your message more effectively.

At exactly that moment he realised that he had been neglecting his youngest daughter.

Should I have a full script?

You should do whatever works for you. Some people print everything out, others have note-cards, and there are some who can memorise their sermons.

Whichever way you choose, the key thing is not to make it obvious. Don't be tied to your notes, and don't tell people you're not using a script (there's no virtue in it). Instead, engage with the congregation, not your pieces of paper.

If you have jokes or illustrations which you can remember well, then these give you short opportunities to leave your manuscript behind. When you are look-ing out, rather than down, you come across so much better.

If you do have to read out what you have written, don't forget to put your oomph into it. If you can't put any oomph into it, then maybe you would be better off printing copies for every-body and handing them out at the end of the service for the congregation to read at home.

Should I speak from the pulpit?

If that's what it takes to get people to vote for Jesus, then so be it. Many churches have a pulpit and a lectern. You can use either, but there may be an expectation that you will stand in the pulpit. If your speech is on the quiet side, a pulpit often helps with voice projection.

If you want to walk around, that's OK too. Try not to be too distracting.

Other practical tips

Do get to the venue early. There are all sorts of things that need sorting out before you speak. Ideally be there at least 30 minutes beforehand. You can then decide where you will speak. You can check out the amplification system. You can take your time to get all your papers in order. You can meet and greet the congregation beforehand. This gives you a better chance of persuading them later, and also allows you to hear of any local news which might inform your preaching. By your early presence, you are also speaking without words about the importance with which you view your task.

If you turn up at the last minute, then you are asking for confusion, which will not help you in your bid to persuade people to vote for Jesus.

At the end of the service, it is always good to shake hands with the congregation as they leave. You will get all kinds of comments, good, bad and totally thoughtless. This is a last opportunity to get people to vote for Jesus just before they head out to the polling station of everyday life. Be sincere and encouraging.

If anybody wants to talk to you about what you said, then gentle debate is fine, but don't attack them! Some people will never be persuaded. Try to spend your time with the 'swing voters' – those people who might go either way – rather than with those who agree with your every word, or those who think you're entirely wrong.

What about preaching in the open air?

This is a different technique again, requiring even more energy. In the open air your stage is wider so you have to put in more oomph than ever. The attention span of your congregation will be shorter, so you have to work harder at drawing them in.

You are also more likely to get involved in dialogue. In other words, you are going to be heckled. The advice about graciousness, in Chapter 8, remains but any open-air preacher needs a thick skin and a quick wit.

Choose your pitch well, and go where you can be heard by the maximum number of people for the greatest impact. Take a few friends with you.

Speak clearly and carefully. Don't be rude to your audience. If you can use humour, so much the better.

St Paul and me

Everywhere St Paul preached, he was followed either by great riots or great revival. Everywhere I preach I'm followed by tea and biscuits . . .

Having said that, nobody's ever fallen out of the window during one of my sermons . . .

Chapter 10

Younger voters

Children can learn to vote for Jesus too! They may not be able to vote for Jesus in the way adults do, but they can be persuaded by sermons.

When you do preach to children, all the lessons learnt in previous chapters apply – only more so. The structure has to allow re-entry into the sermon because children tend to 'dip in and out' even more than adults. The language to be used needs extra care.

Seven questions that children ask

- Where did I come from?
- Who created God?
- Why is Jesus nice, but God so scary?
- How do you think of your sermons?
- Why does the eldest inherit everything (especially when the questioner is not the eldest child)?
- Why did God kill the firstborn in Egypt (especially when the questioner is the eldest child)?
- Why did God kill all the animals when Noah built the ark? That's not fair.

Children have questions, just like adults. Their inquisitive, questioning nature is more receptive to the real gospel than the closed world of adulthood can be. For those who think they already know all the answers, the questions of children can be both revealing and challenging. To a child, some of the things in the world that adults accept without thinking, like inequality and poverty, seem outrageous.

Younger children (under 12) find decision-making difficult. But teenagers are ready to question, and to make up their own minds on the issues.

If you can encourage children to vote for Jesus now, then hopefully they will also continue to vote for Jesus in the years to come.

The approach whereby questions are asked and answered in worship is ideal, because children are always asking questions. If you can model a faith that is not afraid to ask questions, then in those difficult teenage years, when everything is questioned, there is less chance of long-term rejection.

When faith is like an egg, solid enough in normal circumstances but ready to crack when under pressure, it won't last long.

When faith is robust enough to be poked and prodded and examined from every angle, it might be squashed and bent out of shape, but it can still last.

The results of not preaching to children

If children never hear a sermon, but stay out of church and go to their own classes, then they never learn to appreciate a sermon. They learn instead that children are different, and that sermons are for adults. Church worship becomes a foreign activity. When the time comes for them to leave the Sunday School and join the church, they have no experience of what goes on, so it all comes as a great surprise. This is why the Confirmation of teenagers is often seen as a graduation from the church. The young people are now expected to stay in for the sermon – before long they find they have better things to do on a Sunday morning. They have not learnt the art of listening to a sermon.

An excellent book to read is *You Can Preach to the Kids Too* by Carolyn Brown (see Chapter 13).

Chapter 11

The latest technology

Preparation

Some people know their Bibles really well after years of study. For the rest of us, there is the concordance, where you can look up particular words and find out which Bible verses they were in.

This used to be quite a skilled task, but today with CD-ROMS and a PC, it is very easy indeed. If you were thinking of preaching on the issue of suffering, you would search in your PC Bible (or on the Internet) for the word *suffer** – any word beginning with the letters 'suffer'. In the New International Version of the Bible, my computer found 127 references. Not all of them are suitable by any means, but this is a good place to start. Looking for the word 'pain' found a further 37.

You might well choose to speak using one of these texts, but you would use some of the others to inform what you had to say. You couldn't use all of them without losing clarity.

By studying the development of thought on suffering in the Bible, you can trace the simplistic 'You must have done something bad to be suffering' through the more thoughtful 'Why are bad things happening to good people?' and on to 'The Son of Man must suffer many things'.

There will be people in your congregation who hold themselves responsible for their own suffering. You can give them a simple yet profound message about how suffering is not a punishment, and how Jesus is on our side during our pain.

In the same way there are several on-line commentaries you can access on the Internet. These give you background information about passages in the Bible.

The use of computers means that research that once took hours now takes minutes. Use all the resources at your disposal.

Proclamation

There are very few places today outside the church where you would go to hear a person speak without any visual aids.

Even in the most unsophisticated venue, you would expect at the least an overhead projector, or a video recorder, and you would hope for a computerised PowerPoint presentation.

Each of these can have their place in the sermon. You want to persuade people to vote for Jesus as best you can, and it is certainly not cheating to use all the means at your disposal.

The model described in Chapter 6, of coming back to a repeated phrase, can be used particularly effectively – whatever digressions are made from the main topic, when you come back, there is the main theme again, lit up on the screen. Anyone who has wandered from the topic in the last few minutes is in no doubt that we are back on schedule.

In lieu of attending our small groups this Wednesday, we will all be meeting in the chat area of our website @www.thischurch.com

Remember, if you are going to use copyright material, such as a scene from a film or the words of a poem, then you will need a licence to do so.

Have contingency plans if the audio fails or the bulb goes on the projector. The lone voice has less likelihood of going wrong (although there is usually a glass of water for the preacher in case it does).

If it means that people will vote for Jesus, then use modern technology. In itself, however, it is neither necessary nor sufficient.

You *can* get people to vote for Jesus with the spoken word alone, and remember the comments about depth in Chapter 6. Sometimes less is more.

It is not *sufficient* to have the latest technology if you have nothing to say. You can have a beautiful presentation, but without that call to persuade, it is no more than a resounding gong, or a clanging cymbal, or even a reflecting screen.

Content is very important, and everything in your display must be subordinate to your aim of encouraging people to vote for Jesus. It would be a great shame if at the end of the service people complimented your presentation rather than acted upon what you said.

Chapter 12 —— From curious canvasser —————— to convinced candidate?

You've got a passion to change the world, and you have something to say. You've been practising your voice exercises and speaking in public. You're ready to go – what happens next?

In most denominations there is the opportunity to get involved in preaching. Go to see your minister, and talk about your call. Not everybody is called to preaching, but the very fact that you're reading this book suggests that you have at least an inkling that it might be for you.

You have to start somewhere, and you may as well start today. My first sermon contained everything I'd ever thought about in Christianity. It went from Genesis to Revelation and back again. I hope I've improved since!

If you do test your call, then it is a lifelong journey of discovery. You can always improve your preaching. Never be complacent.

Take every opportunity to learn.

Old hands

If you are an established preacher then there is a challenge for you as well.

Most preachers I have talked to consider themselves to be above average. By the laws of mathematics only half of them can be right. As a person who has bought this book, you are well on the way to becoming above average, because the best preachers know their own limitations and are always striving to find new ways to get the message across. The very fact that you are seeking to better your preaching is a good sign. Keep learning.

Convincing

Whether you are a new preacher or old, I hope that in this book I have convinced you of three things:

1. the importance of preaching
2. the validity of the 'question' model of sermon
3. the need to be relevant

The only way to find out whether it all really works is to put it into practice, and to have a go yourself. What's stopping you from trying it next time you preach?

May God bless you as you try to persuade people to vote for Jesus.

Manifestos

Preaching

The Soul Winner
C. H. Spurgeon (Eerdmans,
ISBN 0 8028 8081 9)

An Evangelical Theology of Preaching
Donald English (Abingdon Press,
ISBN 0687 121787)

The Joy of Preaching
Phillips Brooks (Kregel Publications,
ISBN 08254 22760)

www.preaching.com – Lectionary
resources on the Internet

Children

The Runaway Bunny
Margaret Wise Brown (HarperTrophy,
ISBN 0064430189)

*You Can Preach to the Kids Too:
Designing Sermons for Adults and
Children*, Carolyn C. Brown
(Abingdon Press, ISBN 0 687 06157 1)

Practical

Your Voice and How to Use It
Cicely Berry (Virgin Publishing,
ISBN 0863698263)

General

Getting it Across
Nick Fawcett (Kevin Mayhew,
ISBN 1 84003 409 2)

Quotes and Anecdotes
Anthony P. Castle (Kevin Mayhew,
ISBN 0 86209 558 1)

More Quotes and Anecdotes
Anthony P. Castle (Kevin Mayhew,
ISBN 0 86209 932 3)

Quips and Quotes
H. J. Richards (Kevin Mayhew,
ISBN 1 84003 094 1)

More Quips and Quotes
H. J. Richards (Kevin Mayhew,
ISBN 1 84003 667 2)

Apologetic

Mere Christianity, C. S. Lewis
(Fount, ISBN 0006280544)

Worship

Cooking Up Worship
David E. Flavell (Kevin Mayhew,
ISBN 1 84003 375 4)

Cooking Up Worship

A practical resource for creating simple but profound worship

David E. Flavell

Christian worship is exciting, innovative and life-changing – or at least that's what it should be. If your church isn't like that, then you need this book.

Too often the church is like a restaurant whose clientele is dwindling because the chef doesn't seem to care what the customer wants. What's on offer is stodgy, dull and unattractive.

David Flavell makes no apology for being controversial in his assessment of the present state of affairs but goes on to provide constructive, well-presented and easily understood guidelines for cooking up services that are attractive and give glory to God. There is no need for a degree in theology, music or cuisine; the requirements are the desire to reach people where they are and at the same time to please God – simple but profound.

If you have enjoyed *Vote for Jesus*, then you're sure to like *Cooking Up Worship*, the companion volume.

Available from Kevin Mayhew Ltd.

Product Code: 1500275
ISBN: 1 84003 375 4